THE GENERAL

THE GENERAL

The ordinary man who became one of the
bravest prisoners in Guantánamo

AHMED ERRACHIDI WITH GILLIAN SLOVO

Chatto & Windus
LONDON

Published by Chatto & Windus 2013

2 4 6 8 10 9 7 5 3 1

First published in Great Britain in 2013 by
Chatto & Windus
Random House, 20 Vauxhall Bridge Road,
London SW1V 2SA
www.vintage-books.co.uk

Addresses for companies within The Random House Group Limited can be found at:
www.randomhouse.co.uk/offices.htm

The Random House Group Limited Reg. No. 954009

A CIP catalogue record for this book
is available from the British Library

ISBN 9780701187224

The Random House Group Limited supports The Forest Stewardship Council
(FSC®), the leading international forest certification organisation. Our books carrying
the FSC label are printed on FSC® certified paper. FSC is the only forest certification
scheme endorsed by the leading environmental organisations, including Greenpeace.
Our paper procurement policy can be found at www.randomhouse.co.uk/environment

Typeset by Palimpsest Book Production Ltd, Falkirk, Stirlingshire
Printed and bound in Great Britain by Clays Ltd, St Ives plc

This book is dedicated to my dear mother, who has suffered so greatly from what was done to her son; my lovely wife, who lost her other half for so many years; my sons Mohammed and Imran, my daughter Hanan, my niece Imane and all the members of our family who experienced the pain of our separation.

This book is also dedicated to the free people of this world whose words of support and solidarity gave me strength, helping me to understand that I was not alone.

And finally, I dedicate this book to all prisoners of injustice and torture around the world, but especially to my brothers who are still being unjustly held in Guantánamo, and the families of the prisoners who lost their lives there.

Introduction

As a daughter of two of South Africa's prominent anti-apartheid activists, I learned from an early age what sudden police raids and detention without trial looked like in close-up. In 1963 my mother, Ruth First, was held in solitary confinement under South Africa's notorious ninety-day detention without trial laws, an experience that took her to the brink of suicide. After her release, and after we'd settled in Britain, she wrote about her time in jail. Echoes of this returned when, in 2004, I was commissioned to write a verbatim play, *Guantánamo*, for the Tricycle Theatre in Kilburn.

We knew little then about America's offshore prison. There were those few iconic images of kneeling men, handcuffed in orange overalls, their faces hidden by masks and earmuffs, but the identities of the prisoners the Bush administration called the worst of the worst, and the circumstances in which they'd been picked up as well as the conditions under which they were being held, were shrouded in mystery. I set out with the journalist Victoria Brittain to interview the families of the incarcerated as well as lawyers like Clive Stafford Smith (about whom Ahmed writes here) who were among the few civilians to have eventually been given access to the detainees. We heard accounts that seemed at first unlikely, then preposterous and finally, astonishingly, true. We heard, for example, of the journey of British resident Bisher al Rawi who, having been seized by the Americans from the Gambia where he'd gone on business, ended up on that little bit of America at the edge of Cuba. Or the Kafkaesque journey of British citizen Jamal Al-Harith who, having been imprisoned by the Taliban under suspicion of being a British spy and then released after the Taliban fled, was subsequently taken to Guantánamo and kept there for over two years.

As I was writing the play, the first group of British detainees, who included Jamal Al-Harith, were let out of Guantánamo. When their release was announced, there was an emergency meeting of our team to discuss whether we should stop the project because we assumed that the whole sorry episode would soon be over. The irony of it: even now, a full eight years later, and despite Barack Obama's pre-election promise to close the prison camp, 171 prisoners still remain in Guantánamo.

In 2011, when the Moroccan-born chef Ahmed Errachidi, who'd been held in Guantánamo for over five years, was looking for someone to help him complete his book, my play made me an obvious person to approach. I read his manuscript, which had been written in Arabic and then translated, and, at least in the beginning, I read it as a courtesy to someone who had suffered so greatly. By then pressure from the British government had led to the release of most of the British residents who had been held in Guantánamo (none of whom were subsequently charged) and so conditions in the prison camp were better documented. Because of this, I didn't expect to learn much that was new from Ahmed's account. I was wrong. I found myself reading with growing interest. By the time I reached the end of his draft I was surprised by how moved I was and surprised by the portrait of resistance that had unfolded. Intrigued, I agreed to fly out to Tangier to meet him.

A solid mountain of a man, Ahmed Errachidi likes to cook

and he also likes to eat. On our first day together, we drove for hours in his 4x4 in search of a restaurant that he particularly wanted to take me to. All the time he drove he talked, and the more he talked the slower he drove, so it was late afternoon before we were finally sitting at a table. His subjects were twofold: his religion and his time in Guantánamo, and these, I began to realise, were intimately connected. Although he was a practising Muslim when he was picked up, Guantánamo made him more observant. Ask him about his growing faith and he will wryly admit that his past behaviour contains many errors. Yet now, he says, his faith is strong, and his determination to lead a morally upright life informs almost everything he does. This is a result of Guantánamo: during his incarceration a conviction that Allah was testing him and that, if he survived this test, everything would turn out all right, is what sustained him.

For a man who was held without charge for over five years, and who spent much of that time in solitary, Ahmed seems to be in remarkably good shape. A family man, he talks passionately about his three children. His weekends are spent ferrying the wider family to the beach (picnics his responsibility, food elaborately described), and his weeks preparing the start-up of his own restaurant. The most visible signs of the privation he endured are his edginess in confined spaces (he always wanted to talk outside) and the strange timbre of his voice. As I listened to him I noticed that although he can pitch his voice low and he can also pitch it high – he appears to have no middle range. 'It never used to be like this,' he tells me. 'It happened in Guantánamo: too much shouting maybe, or too much gas spray.' Asked whether he has consulted a doctor, he says, 'I did. But he wanted to put something down my throat to see what is happening. After what I'd witnessed in Guantánamo of the aftermath of force-feeding, I couldn't face it. I didn't tell the doctor where I'd been, I just said no. I told him, give me antibiotics and I took them. But they didn't help.'

All this is related without a trace of self-pity. As I got to know him better, I began to realise that Ahmed had written his memoir and felt strongly about getting it published not so that the world would feel sorry for him, but so that people would understand what their governments had done in the name of democracy. He seems to feel little rancour for the ordinary soldiers who shackled and sprayed and beat him – he talks about them as ignorant, and he says that were he to meet them again he would try and help them see the errors of their ways. He feels very differently about the men – the Bushes, the Cheneys and the Rumsfelds – who were in charge. Their actions, he insists, were a fundamental attack on democracy for which they should be held accountable: he is passionate about getting the world to understand this.

Our scratchiest moments came when I asked him about al-Qaeda or about a man like Abu Qatada. Not because Ahmed backs either – he made it clear that he abhors the killing of innocents and he'd neither met nor heard of Qatada while in England – but because he didn't want to have to prove his innocence by continual condemnation of al-Qaeda atrocities. As far as he is concerned great wrong was done on 11 September 2001, but this wrong does not cancel out another: the detention without trial and torture of hundreds of men in a lawless Guantánamo. 'Why,' he asked me, 'should I always have to prove that I do not like bin Laden? He's nothing to do with me.'

There were other moments, also, of contestation. At one point I questioned a section of his manuscript where, in describing how he used to talk to his guards about their religious beliefs, he seemed to be equating a belief in Father Christmas with a belief in Jesus as the son of God. I suggested that this might be offensive to Christians and that perhaps he should leave it out. He was happy to take my advice but before we cut the passage he wanted me to know that it had also occurred to him that his arguments might cause offence, but he'd kept them in because, in the strange mindset of Guantánamo, this was how he had talked to the soldiers: and the one thing he'd been determined to do in his account was tell the truth. I listened to what he had to say. And then we kept the passage in.

In our conversations, my experience of Ahmed was of a man trying his utmost to be truthful. Just as he was willing to talk openly about a mental breakdown he'd had in London, he also answered every one of my awkward questions with forbearance and, as far as I could make out, honesty. Only twice did he ask me to leave out something that he'd told me. The first time it was because he was worried that should his sons read it, a personal detail might adversely affect the way they were growing up. The second time was when, because of what they had been through, he was reluctant to criticise the way some of his fellow prisoners had negotiated with the prison administration.

Ahmed is a generous man. He insisted on paying for every meal we shared and on sending me back with presents for my daughter. And when a mutual acquaintance had her computer hacked and everybody in her address book got a bogus request to send her money, Ahmed sent the whole amount. Told that it had all been a hoax, he didn't rant about the cruelty of strangers but instead expressed his relief that his friend hadn't needed the money because that meant she was not in trouble.

This open-heartedness doesn't make Ahmed a pushover. I was to meet the steel in him when, on our second meeting, I tried to turn on my tape recorder. 'Please don't,' he said. 'I see a tape recorder and I dry up.' I tried to persuade him – it was much easier for me to catch his voice and way of speaking if I could play it back – but gently he persisted and eventually, knowing of the scrutiny he'd endured in Guantánamo, I gave in. Our bargain was that he would talk slowly and stop as soon as I asked him to, so I could write down his exact words: it was a bargain he kept to. I say I gave in but, looking back, so persistent was he, I'm not sure I had much of a choice. That one exchange gave me first-hand experience of how determined Ahmed can be, and how hard to budge.

This same determination runs through his book. For *The General* is less a story of the injustice done to one man – although that is certainly here – and more an account of how a man in the most powerless of situations fights to change the balance of power.

That he was an English speaker instantly put Ahmed in the Guantánamo firing line. Yet he could have chosen to step back and, if he had, he would have had an easier time of it. But his fierce pride and his resolve to stand up to injustice meant that he didn't choose the easy way. That's why he ended up spending so much time in solitary and perhaps also why he seems to have survived so well. The result is a book which is not just a catalogue of injustices but a testimony to the way an ordinary man can find in himself an extraordinary will to resist.

Gillian Slovo
May 2012

1

They'd strapped goggles over my eyes so all I could see, through the gap on the bridge of my nose, was a small section of my feet. They'd also made me wear earmuffs, and a thick paper mask, and mittens made from material so stiff I couldn't move my fingers and which cut off the circulation to my hands. And, on top of this, they'd shoved in a suppository that stopped me needing the toilet, and sprayed my head with a chemical that I could still feel burning through my skin. And then they had put me on first one plane and then another.

There I sat on the second plane on a low bench between two other prisoners. We were in intimate proximity – I could feel their arms and legs touching mine – but since communication was forbidden and I couldn't see them, I had no idea who they were. We were chained together, our legs shackled to rings on the floor and to each other, while another horizontal chain joined us by our waists along the line. And so we sat, motionless, through a journey that felt like it was never going to end. Later I was able to figure out that the whole transfer took roughly twenty-six hours, during which time we were kept blindfolded, muffled, chained and motionless.

It was the worst experience of my life. Forbidden to move, and cramped for such an extended period, I began to experience the most terrible pains. They shot, jagged, through my joints making me want to cry out, although I'd learned that if I did I'd only earn myself a beating.

I'd been a prisoner of the Americans for long enough to know that they were moving me to a prison in Cuba where the rules of law didn't apply.

I didn't care where I was headed or what awful fate might befall me there. All I wanted was to be allowed to shift my weight so as to relieve the pain or, if that wasn't possible, to die. I prayed for the end, either of this journey or of my life. I was in such pain that the only way I could make myself feel better was imagining that this was the Day of Judgement. And then at last I heard the muffled roar of the engines changing and I felt the plane beginning its descent.

It took an agonisingly long time before I finally felt the glorious jolt of wheels touching down. I heard a door opening and the sounds of boots, and the clang of chains as they unhooked us from the plane. Then we were ordered out, shuffling forward in our shackles and guided by commands. I was so relieved to be on my feet and so accustomed to having men I didn't know push me about: I went where I was told to go. I could smell the salty tang of the sea wafting in on a breeze that stirred the humid air. I followed the line of prisoners in front of me onto some kind of vehicle – I think it was a boat because I could feel it shifting sideways – and like them I knelt, something that I, a large man, have always found difficult. After what I reckoned must have been about an hour we were told to get up and move out, and then once again ordered onto our knees. I could hear a man, he must have been an American because he had an awkward accent, telling us in Arabic not to move. The pain returned as my weight pressed down on knees that felt ready to crack. To try and relieve the pressure, I shifted to one side. Someone belted me, twice, against the back of my head. 'Don't move,' a harsh voice shouted. 'Don't move.'

I couldn't take it. I fell forward. In that moment before I lost consciousness I thought back to my childhood and to what I might have done to deserve this terrible fate.

I am Moroccan and was born in Tangier in 1966, the middle of five children. In Guantánamo I did a lot of thinking back to my early life and one of the people I thought about most was my father whose behaviour and example had a great impact on me.

He was a farmer, a strong man, and very tall, very upstanding. He did everything for us children, and he was also incredibly kind. Only once, when I was seven, did he ever hit me. I'd insulted a farmer who was poorer than us and my father, who was bringing us up to respect all people no matter how poor they were, got so angry when he heard what I'd done that he slapped me. But because he was also a gentle man who never usually resorted to violence, he couldn't bear to see me upset. When I started to cry, he gave me money for an ice lolly. That was my father all over: a mixture of softness and absolute propriety.

He'd had a tough childhood: his mother had died when he was young and his father had remarried someone who didn't like him so he'd left home prematurely. As a result, although he had gone to traditional religious classes, he'd not got as far as learning to read or write. So he taught himself, buying books until we had a small library at home – mostly religious books, guides about how to pray and how to fast.

I loved my father very much and as a child I was always at his side. I loved to hear his stories that were filled with challenge, heroism and defiance. Remembering them in Guantánamo, I wonder whether they helped to build my own determination.

The story I best remember dates back to the 1940s and it goes like this: my father was one of a number of young men digging the foundations for a hotel in Tangier in the heat of the day. He was so strong he could work his shovel with one hand, even when he reached the hard earth two metres down. But my father didn't stay long in that particular job because soon after he'd started working there the man in charge, who was Italian, became abusive, shouting 'Come on, you donkeys' to the men working the foundations. At this my father downed his shovel and climbed out. When the Italian demanded to know where he thought he was going, my father just said: 'I don't work with donkeys,' and left. He soon found another job – there were plenty of opportunities in those days – but after a while the Italian tracked my father and his legendary strength down and asked him to come and get rid of a massive rock in his garden which was getting in the way of his entertaining. My father didn't want to work for such an abusive man but the Italian dared him to prove that he was the man he pretended to be, and my father would never refuse such a challenge, especially when there was mockery involved. So he agreed to take a look at the rock.

When he got to the garden he saw how enormous the rock was. As the Italian sneered to further provoke him, my father stayed calm. He walked round the rock. He climbed it, ignoring the Italian's escalating scorn, and he examined it all over. Then at last he said: 'I'll take on this challenge.' What my father and nobody else had noticed was that this was not one but two rocks sealed together by time and that there was a small, almost invisible, fissure running between the two. All my father need do was to get his hammer and pick, place the pick on the line and hammer until the rock split, and then he could work on the fragments until they were small enough to be carted away. When the job was done, the Italian was so impressed by my father's strength and guile he wanted to keep him in his pay. But my father told him that he'd only come for the challenge, and that he'd never work for a man who insults his employees.

This story stuck in my memory, especially when my father kept repeating how much he had wanted to prove to the Italian that he was not a donkey but a man. I admired that in my father. From a very early age, I wanted to grow up fast to prove myself a man just like him. Little did I know that it would take the privations of Guantánamo for me to understand that I was strong enough to endure and resist even the most terrible abuse.

I look back on my childhood with great nostalgia. My father had a plot of about two hectares that was five minutes from where we lived in Tangier. It was close to the shore in what was once the outskirts of the city. It had four wells and fig trees – and my father used to grow vegetables there, enough for him to sell. Now that land has been tarred over and turned into a big parking space for people who are waiting to take the ferry to Europe. I look at this, sometimes, and feel the irony of it. But in those days it was a small, working farm, where my father also kept some cows, employing several people to help him. Our neighbours would come and pick vegetables before showing their baskets so my father could tally up how much they owed. He was very generous and especially kind to those less well off than him. He would often look into a full basket and then say to the impoverished woman holding it, 'Don't worry about paying: go quick and make your vegetable pot.' People treated him with great respect, they called him *sharif*, meaning someone who is honoured and who has dignity.

I was always trying to make him proud of me, and when I was young, I spent all the time I could working on the farm. My ambition was to grow up to be his right-hand man. It was actually quite hard to keep up with him. Farming was not his only income: he was skilled in a number of trades and he worked such long hours that I don't remember him ever spending a whole day at home. Even during festivals like Eid he'd go out and work. When my mother told him to rest, he'd say he wanted to provide us with everything we needed. I'd sit up, way after my brothers and sisters had gone to sleep, and wait for him to come home. When he did, my mother would tell him that all the children had eaten and gone to bed – all except Ahmed. She'd serve him supper

11

and he'd invite me to join him. Concerned that my mother might have prepared a better meal than the one she'd given us, he'd insist that I share his.

Throughout my childhood I kept hold of this adoration for my father and whenever I was with him I felt the warmth of his love for me. When I was in Guantánamo, thoughts of him, the smell of his farm and of Tangier sustained me. I especially liked to remember the end of spring when the hot air of the coming summer would begin to dry out the succulent grass. That scent of fresh grass evaporating is one I love because it throws me right back to my childhood on the farm. And it tended to be spring that I most set my mind on in Guantánamo, remembering the brightness of bougainvillea, the sweetness of jasmine and the sticky yellow of mimosa to help me survive.

Before I started school I used to go to a playgroup where one of the boys, who was older than me, had such a bad stutter that he struggled to enunciate a single word. Aged five I envied this stutter because it made the boy different, special, which is what I wanted to be. I used to go and sit under an electricity pylon near the farm and practise stuttering. There I'd stay, unseen for an hour or two, stuttering away until eventually I learned how to do it without trying. I never told anyone what I was up to and when, after I'd started school, my teacher asked my mother where I'd picked up my stutter, my mother had no idea. I still stutter to this day, especially when I am nervous. Perhaps the electricity has forged its pattern inside me.

I went to school when I was seven, and we were taught in Arabic and in French. The school wasn't far from where we lived, and then there was only sand and a railway track between the school and the sea. During the breaks we used to cross the track so we could eat our olive sandwiches by the seashore. I did well at school and particularly at composition: I won prizes and my work was read out nearly every week. I told myself then that one day I'd write a book. I could never have dreamed that this would be the one.

I was an adventurous and determined boy, always trying to do things for myself. One incident I remember will tell you something about the child I was: it took place before I'd started school, so I must have been about six. My mother had taken me and my brothers to a funfair which I so enjoyed I wanted to go again. I knew my mother probably wouldn't take me a second time and so, without asking permission, I decided to go on my own. I planned my trip carefully, putting on my best clothes before setting off. I didn't know exactly where the funfair was so I just headed for the lights. I must have walked more than two kilometres to get there. It was an unusual thing to do. In those days, we children, brought up as we were on stories about gangs and kidnappings, never went anywhere on our own.

I reached the fair but having no money I couldn't ride the carousel, or go on a car, or a plane, or eat candyfloss, as I would have done had I been with my mother. But I was happy enough roaming around, taking in all the wonderful sights. I was having so much fun, in fact, that I didn't register time passing until at last it dawned on me that everything had quietened down and that almost everyone else had left. The fair was closing: it was past time for me to go home. But by now I was scared of the dark and the empty streets.

It hadn't occurred to me to worry about the upset my compassionate mother would feel when she realised I was gone. Later I learned how her heart almost flew away in panic. She'd always tried to hide my naughtiness from my father and now she couldn't bring herself to tell him that she didn't know where I was. She knew he'd react badly about what had happened and blame her for it. So she served him dinner, extra hot to slow him down, and told him she needed urgently to visit my aunt who lived close by. Soon my aunt had my cousin and a neighbour out scouring the place. They found me wandering around in the darkness and so my mother was able to get me home before my father had even finished his meal.

Years later in my cell, with a lot of time on my hands to ponder and analyse my life, I'd look back on this incident as an early indication of a particular combination of independence, determination and the desire to have what I wanted. This desire was fed in adolescence when I'd go to the movies as often as I could. I'd look at the hero, and I'd see how he always seemed to have a car, a house, and how he would come into that house and open the fridge and fill it with groceries. I wanted that life. I wanted to be independent of my family and to afford the kind of goods I kept seeing on the silver screen. I really believed that to achieve this heart's desire all I needed to do was go north, to Europe. It's funny to think of it now because of course these were all American movies that had been translated into French. So I was dreaming of an American lifestyle, not one I'd find in Europe.

There was a hill near our home where I often used to sit, gazing out to sea. I loved the sense of space there and the vastness of the horizon. At nights I'd stare at the dancing lights of Spain and Gibraltar. I'd watch them for hours and promise myself that one day I'd cross over to them.

2

There were a lot of tourists in Tangier and I soon became their little guide. I'd show them the sights, mixing with these blonde, light-skinned people, chatting with them, practising my few words of English. I still have the pictures I took of them. One couple who lived in Chesterfield invited me to come and visit. Of course, this only made me yearn to travel more. I was in a race with the future. I thought I'd become a man by travelling. I wanted to earn and spend my own money rather than let my parents tell me what to do. I had also promised my mother that one day I'd buy her everything her heart desired and this is something I was absolutely determined to do.

At eighteen when I became eligible for a passport I immediately applied for one. I told my father that, despite my successes at school, I was planning to travel to London, which I'd had postcards of and wanted to see for myself. I wanted to try living in another country, and I told my parents this. I was looking for a new life, a whole new set of experiences. So even though I knew I was only eligible for a holiday visa, I told my parents I was going to emigrate.

My father was upset – he couldn't bear the thought of me

living so far away – and he tried to convince me to stay with him in Morocco. Eighteen years old was much younger and more inexperienced in those days than it is today, and he was afraid for me. But, eventually, realising I was adamant, he gave in. He wished me all good luck and success, his only proviso being that he couldn't witness my departure. And so it was that in the summer of 1985, I bid farewell to every member of my family except my father. Even after I'd settled in London, when I called home I'd speak to everyone but him. One day when I asked them to get him to the phone, he burst into tears, crying so hard at the sound of my voice that he couldn't say a word.

I felt such guilt about the pain I was causing him but I wanted so much to travel that I didn't listen. I don't think this is so unusual: I think all mankind yearns to see other places. Curiosity to know more of the world is in our nature, and in those days many young men like me also travelled to Europe and learned about other peoples and other ways of life first-hand. This is no longer possible for people like us – there's such a distrust of Muslims that our young men can only go to places like Afghanistan and Pakistan and that changes their ideas. I met such a young man in Guantánamo, there only because he'd wanted to go on holiday.

I took a boat to Spain, a train through France and then, from Calais, another boat to Folkestone where I was given one month's visa. I found my way to Chesterfield and to the couple who'd invited me to visit. I spent a few days with them before going to London where I stayed in a tent city in east Acton. I rented a bunk bed for £2 a night, sharing with people from all over Europe and from places further afield like South Africa. I liked London. Despite the clouds, I took to the climate. I even liked it when it was dark and rainy and I couldn't catch the vaguest glimpse of the sun. And I found it easy to interact with British people. They gave me my privacy, my space. Although it was a foreign place to me, I was allowed to do what I wanted.

I stayed in London for a couple of weeks. I had a good time

taking in the Western way of life just as I'd wanted to. But I was running out of money, so I decided to go to Scotland where I thought I might find work. I was so young and so naive. I set off hitchhiking without really knowing where I was going. The first lorry driver who picked me up laughed his head off when I told him where I wanted to go – he said it was too far away – but he did take me to a petrol station where I was picked up by an Iraqi driver who offered to drive me as far as Sheffield. We got to talking and the Iraqi tried to persuade me to go home – life in England was tough, he said, and cold and I'd be better off going home. I thought I wasn't really listening but when he dropped me off in Sheffield at nightfall and I tried to save money by sleeping out, something I'd not previously done, his advice kept reverberating. The night didn't want to end and I was freezing and suddenly very homesick, missing my mother's calm and care, and wondering what on earth I was doing in England on my own. So I retraced my steps back to London and then to Folkestone, and home.

I stayed in Tangier for a few months but once again found myself sitting on the hill looking out across the sea towards Europe. Now, though, I was filled with regret that my ambition to see more of the rest of the world had been defeated by one cold, sleepless night. I wasn't ready to give up my dream of living in a more prosperous place and so I set off again. I visited Tunisia, Libya, Spain, Malta, France, Belgium and Holland before eventually making my way back to England.

This time I felt more at home and so, when my visa was about to expire, I asked the Home Office for an extension. At first I was refused. But when I pleaded with the official who'd initially said no, he went to consult his supervisor and came back saying they'd give me another month. He stamped my passport – this was in September 1986 – and I left, happy that they'd let me prolong my stay. But when I was on the bus and idly opened my passport to admire my visa extension, I saw that by mistake the official had given me a year and a month. I was over the moon. With a visa, I felt myself in a way to be legal and so I started looking for a job.

I still had very little English. I'd walk into a restaurant and say: 'Excuse me. Hello. Good morning. I am looking for a job' – these were the only sentences I knew. I tried them everywhere and eventually got my first job in a restaurant in Aldgate called Blooms. When the boss spoke to me I'd look into his eyes and try and guess whether I should reply with a yes or a no. If I said yes, and he seemed shocked, I'd then quickly say no.

After that I went to a Beefeater in Tower Hill and finally I got a more permanent job as a kitchen porter in Mayfair. I'd clean dishes, mop the floor, do anything that was asked of me.

My personal life was also flourishing. I'd met an Englishwoman, a hairdresser and a Christian who after our first meeting wrote a poem about me. She lived in Hammersmith; I was in Battersea sharing a two-bedroom flat with three people. I don't remember how long it took us to decide to get married, but I do remember that I'd fallen in love with her – she was in effect my first love – and that she cried when I proposed.

It didn't work out between us partly because, to save money, we went to live with her father and her father didn't like me. I think it's possible that he didn't like his daughter being married to a foreigner. Whatever his reasons, things became so difficult that we broke up.

I came out of the marriage badly. I gave her what she asked for, including money. I loved her and I was hurt but I didn't delay our divorce, which was my legal right to do, even though if I had I'd have had an easier time securing my position in England (I was almost at the point of being able to apply for indefinite leave to remain). The whole experience left me profoundly sad.

Yet still I decided to stay on in England. I liked the country and the people, I liked my freedom and I wasn't ready to go home. By then I was working in a restaurant where every Wednesday the head chef, John, would roast chicken thighs for us workers. My relationship with him was good enough for me to tell him that we were tired of his dry chicken thighs and wanted a change. He challenged me to do better. Since leaving my family in Morocco, I'd been cooking for myself and so I took up his challenge. I cooked the chicken in a pot with potatoes, peas and turmeric, cumin and parsley and tomato purée, lemon, cardamom and bay leaves. The first person to taste my dish was the restaurant manager. When he rang the kitchen phone to praise the food John told him, 'Don't tell me, thank Ahmed. He cooked it.' The manager asked for the name of the dish: since I'd made it up on the spot, I told him, laughingly, 'If you like, call it Ahmed's chicken.' Everyone who ate the dish was full of appreciative comments and John continued to give me the credit. And so it was that, every Wednesday, I'd cook chicken for them and in turn they would wash my dishes.

My life as a cook had begun. It was helped along when John told me that a group of customers wanted a vegetarian meal and he wanted me to cook one of the dishes. I invented a dish of cauliflower, peas, basil, tomatoes, garlic, pepper and cumin onto which I cracked eggs before putting it into the oven. It was a great success. The customers enjoyed all the food but praised mine the most. This gave me the confidence to think that I really could cook well. I lost interest in washing dishes and found a job in a cafe where I cooked simple items such as eggs and hamburgers.

I loved cooking and paid great attention to it: I was very keen on learning the art from other chefs. I moved from restaurant to restaurant which helped me to gain experience in many different styles. I'd no professional qualifications, but even so I made it as far as deputy head chef on more than one occasion.

3

In my years in London I only occasionally went to mosque –
I wasn't a regular. I wasn't what you'd call a hundred-per-cent
practising Muslim. Like many other young men, I'd have phases
where I'd have the best intentions and would pray the requisite
five times a day, but laziness would soon kick in and I'd stop. But
in 1992 something happened which had a massive impact on me
and sent me back to my roots.

It was Ramadan, a time when I'd always go to mosque. I was
with my friend Mohammad, a Moroccan who'd been raised in
London and who I'd met through a mutual friend and had been
immediately drawn to. He's a lovely man and we were the best of
friends. I could often be found eating at his house courtesy of
his hospitable wife, or playing snooker with him, and on one
of his visits to Morocco he'd met my family which forged an
extra connection between us. So on this day we naturally went to
mosque together.

I noticed that Mohammad was behaving oddly but I couldn't
figure out why. He'd driven us there and after prayer, as we sat in
his parked car, he starting talking to me. He asked me all sorts
of, for him, uncharacteristic questions, like whether I believed

God was in charge and whether I agreed that what happened on earth was beyond our control, and each time he asked one of these questions he'd wait for me to answer in the affirmative before asking me the next. I kept saying yes, right until the moment when he asked me to confirm that what happened was God's will. My heart wanted to say yes, but my lips refused to move – perhaps by then I'd guessed what was coming. So I held my tongue.

I looked at Mohammad, waiting for him to speak again but he'd also frozen – later he told me that he'd been on the point of saying what he'd been summoning up the courage to say, but my failure to answer as he'd expected meant he couldn't bear to. And so that evening we parted without his ever getting to the point.

The next day at mosque we met up with two Moroccans who usually lived in Germany and whom we'd got to know on their visit to London. One of these men was from Tangier and I saw Mohammad, who was still behaving oddly, take this man aside and whisper in his ear. I couldn't work out what was going on but it didn't particularly bother me.

After evening prayer the four of us went for a coffee. When I got up to go, the guy from Tangier said: 'I need to talk to you, my friend,' and as soon as he said that, the other two, who'd been sitting at our table, vanished. I was left with a man I barely knew. We sat initially without talking until eventually he began to speak about Tangier, asking me about my family, and in particular about my father. Aha, I thought: he knows my father.

I hadn't seen my father for seven years and I missed him so much. A window of hope opened up: at least I'd be able to talk about my father to someone who knew what a great guy he was. And then, boom: 'Your father has passed away,' he said.

My father was dead, he was already buried, and I'd just had a stranger break the news.

My family hadn't meant it to be like that: knowing that I'd probably take the news badly they'd asked Mohammad to tell me.

That's what he'd been trying to do the previous night. But when I hadn't answered his questions as he'd anticipated, his nerve had failed. He'd decided that the blow would be lessened if the news came from someone who also knew Tangier and the life I'd left.

It was a mistake: it was far more terrible to hear about the death of my father from a near stranger. I felt a deep sense of betrayal as well as the sheer shock of it. I started crying.

Later my family told me how my father had spent his last hours. It was Ramadan and two little girls had come to the door selling coriander for soup. My father bought some bunches, and when they asked for one diram a bunch, he gave them double the amount which was the kind of thing he always did. He laid the coriander on the stairs and left the house, shutting the door. He walked to the cemetery which was two or three minutes away. Neighbours looking from their balconies watched him going and they saw him looking around the cemetery as if examining his new home. And then on his way back he collapsed. He'd had a heart attack. They picked him up and carried him home. That was about ten in the morning. He knew he was going to die, he had spoken to my brothers and asked them to read particular chapters from the Koran and by midday he was dead. As is our custom he was buried by 4 p.m. that day in the same spot around which he'd been looking. All of this I only discovered three to four days later.

I was devastated, particularly because I hadn't seen him for so long. I was desperate to go home but because of my divorce I was having to appeal an order to leave the country. If I'd left then, I wouldn't have been able to come back.

As a result of grief, and also probably because of my isolation from my family, I lost my mind. It didn't happen all at once. At first I was on a strange high and then I just went crazy in the street and ended up being taken to a mental hospital. I'm talking honestly about this because I'm determined to tell the truth, and because I believe I've got nothing to be ashamed of. Many people, in all walks of life including many very successful people, have experienced mental illness. I'm just one of them: I was unable to function normally because I'd lost the man most precious to me in all the world.

In hospital, I couldn't stop thinking about my seven years in London. About my lifestyle and my failed marriage, and about the way that my father had never wanted me to leave Morocco. It was as if all my decisions were laid out in front of me and when I looked at the life that had resulted, I judged it empty, especially when I compared my father's achievements with my lack of them. I felt as if everything was over. It was as if I'd been smoking a cigarette which had been getting shorter and shorter until I'd reached the filter and even that was burning up. I regretted most of my decisions. I knew I couldn't turn back the clock but I desperately wanted to. My mind kept knocking at that door.

The doctors decided I was bipolar. To this day I don't know if they were right: they have to give you a label, don't they? I do know that I'd not felt like that before, and wouldn't again, until I was in Gitmo. And I also know that Haldol, the medication they first prescribed, didn't agree with me. For three months it felt as if the drug kept moving inside of me. I couldn't stop my legs from shaking uncontrollably, twenty-four hours a day. I lost a huge amount of weight, my cheeks hollowed and my face grew unrecognisably gaunt. I couldn't remember the simplest things and I started having seizures. Then, finally, the doctors took notice of my deteriorating condition and changed my medication to Stelazine and the side effects disappeared. I began to regain my shape and my energy.

At the height of my illness I thought I'd never be the same. Then gradually I realised I was actually becoming myself again. I understood that it had been the medication, as much as anything, that had dragged me down into such a dark place. I began to believe that there might be a second chance, and that the clock might really have been turned back. I was able to rebuild my strength and my memories.

I was let out of hospital, at first as a day patient. Walking the streets of London, I thought how much I'd missed life. With the return of my memory, I hoped that my kitchen skills would also come back. At first, because of the medication, I couldn't control my hand movements but I kept on trying. I was at my friend Mohammad's (he had proved to be a wonderful friend, visiting me every single day when I was in hospital) when I first dared to pick up a knife in the kitchen and when I did it was to slice a watermelon. To my surprise my hands were steady enough to do that, and so I continued to practise and soon was visibly improving, able to cook my own meals. After a few weeks, with my confidence growing, I felt like I was coming out of a coma. Still I didn't have the self-assurance to do real restaurant work so I opted for a job in a fish-and-chip shop. It was my way of trying to get back into cooking and it wasn't very successful: the main skill required was to roll chips up in a paper cone and I was too slow at the folding. I only managed a few days before the owner sacked me.

I decided I should look instead for a job in a proper restaurant and I found one – Casper's in Soho where there were two chefs in charge. I was to be the third under them. I was so pleased to be back in a real kitchen. When I was asked to make a new hollandaise sauce because one had curdled, I impressed the chef in charge by putting the curdled sauce in a stainless-steel bowl over some water that I'd set to boil and then whisked so quickly the sauce reassembled. When the chefs saw that I could do this they started trusting me. I was tasked with making the soups and the chilli with chunks of meat. When the manager tasted my chilli and said that this is how he always wanted it to be, I knew I'd made it back.

4

My father had died in 1992. In 1993 I went back to Tangier for a visit.

Although my father was no longer there, I was, and still am, full of love for my mother. When I got home, I discovered that she'd had a cold for a long time and couldn't seem throw it off so I took her to a private doctor. Without a moment's thought this doctor told her she had a disease in her lungs for which there was no cure. He was right about the disease, she has this infection in her lungs even to this day, but she is still, thank God, alive. But the careless manner in which he broke the news meant that instead of understanding that what he meant was that she had a long-term illness, my mother thought he was telling her that her condition was terminal. I jumped in to correct him, and he did take back his words, but it was too late: my mother kept on thinking she was going to die imminently.

I tried to distract her by asking if she remembered how I'd once promised that when I grew up I'd buy her everything she desired – jewellery, clothes, foods, the lot. When she said she did, I told her that today was the day. But now my poor mother assumed that I was only doing this because the doctor was right, and she really was going to die. Nothing I could do would dissuade her. Even so, I did take her shopping, and bought her clothes, and then, at the food markets, I bought her everything she wanted, along with a gorgeous display of roses. A woman in the market, noticing what was going on, asked my mother: who is this young man? When my mother said I was her son, the lady commented on what a pleasant, obedient boy I was before asking whether I was married. When my mother said no, the lady said she would be pleased if we'd pay her a visit and she gave my mother the address. My mother thought the lady must have daughters to marry off. It cheered her up, filling her with hope, and fixing the damage the doctor's thoughtlessness had wrought.

I was feeling ready to move on, to get married, and have a child. My sister told me about a woman she'd met who'd impressed her by withstanding insults from an older relative, staying calm and polite and not retaliating. I liked the sound of this and asked to meet the woman, whose name was Rahma. I also liked her and soon we were married. It would be one of the best decisions of my life. Rahma is a wonderful wife and mother and I love her dearly. She has stood by me through all my absences, facing much uncertainty and hardship, and yet has always been there for me.

After we married, I tried to start a small business in Morocco but I'd spent so long in London that I couldn't seem to find my way. I'd absorbed so much of English culture and at a formative time in my life, it had changed my way of being and at times I even felt more English than Moroccan. There was so much I'd learned in England – how to talk the language, how to cook, how to drive: it's where I felt most at home. So I left Tangier again, and after that travelled between the two countries; getting to Europe on tourist visas and then crossing over to England, working there illegally, although that never stopped me from getting a job, and then returning home via France. Even after my first son, Mohammad, was born in 1996, I kept travelling between the two countries, seeing my family in Tangier and cooking and making money in London.

My cooking career went from strength to strength. In 1997 I was working as sous chef in a Mediterranean restaurant named Santuria under a skilled English head chef called Chris. He went to Thailand for a holiday and stayed three months and, during his absence, I ran the kitchen. I began by cooking the restaurant's staple dishes and then soon I was making them my own. I used olive oil and green herbs and Mediterranean vegetables such as aubergine, pepper, wild mushrooms, spinach, asparagus, artichokes, baby courgettes as well as various cheeses such as Parmesan, mozzarella and goat's cheese – all normal ingredients, but I found ways of combining them differently, and cooking pastas and risotto which I served with the fresh fish which was our mainstay. I'd always try to combine a large number of items which I knew a particular customer liked into one dish. I'd suggest monkfish or lemon sole or grilled swordfish served on a bed of tagliatelle cooked with ingredients such as spinach and wild mushrooms. The plates would always come back empty.

The best commendation I received was from a man in his seventies. After he'd eaten baked monkfish on a plate of risotto with wild mushrooms, peas, Parmesan, saffron and herbs, he came to the kitchen to say, 'Thank you very much, because it was the best dish of fish that I've ever tasted.' This was quite an acknowledgement from such a venerable source. I took it as a testimony of honour, an apt reward for all my efforts to please our customers. Soon afterwards, another diner came to tell me how much she and her two colleagues had enjoyed the food. It turned out that they were not ordinary diners but food critics. A few days later they sent someone to take pictures of the restaurant and they published an article praising us in the local newspaper. After that we were so busy that by Sunday all our supplies would be finished. And while business usually fell off in August, that August when I was cooking turned out to be the most profitable month of the whole year.

5

I went back to my family in Morocco, staying with them until the birth of my son, Imran, before returning to London to look for more work.

On 11 September 2001 I was sitting with a colleague in a cafe opposite our restaurant in north-west London and, like people all over the world, we watched with disbelief and horror that awful attack unfolding in New York. I couldn't understand why anyone would want to kill all those innocent people. I didn't have the faintest inkling that I'd be caught up in its aftermath, a news item forced to answer the questions of the FBI, CIA and MI5 in Bagram, Kandahar and Guantánamo Bay. What none of us watching our televisions that day could have guessed was that the Bush administration would use the attack as an excuse to kidnap the rule of law.

At this time, in 2001, I was preoccupied by a big personal problem. From a young age our son Imran, who was one-and-a-half by now, had something wrong with his heart, although we didn't know quite what. Now he seemed to be getting worse and I wanted to go and see him, but my legal status (even though I had a lawyer working on my case) still meant that if I left London

I wouldn't be able to return. This brought things to a head. I couldn't keep living between two countries, not with my growing family and my sick son, and, anyway, work had been scarce. It was time to look for an alternative way of making money to provide for my family.

I decided that what I should do was start a business in my own country and build it up. I thought about selling washing-up liquid because in those days in Morocco they still used powder. I contacted companies like Fairy but in the end decided that the product was too expensive. I played with the idea of breeding rabbits – we Moroccans eat rabbits but not in the same quantity as Egyptians and I wondered whether I could change that. But because I didn't have any land I ruled that out as well.

Every Friday after mosque I'd sit in a cafe drinking coffee with other immigrants and one of our most popular topics was always the best way to make money. Different people fed in their ideas and experiences. They talked, for example, about trading silk from China and Turkey or silver from Pakistan. Because I was trying to find a way to go home and stay there while also making money, I listened to these tales with particular attention. The idea of buying silver jewellery in Pakistan felt the most accessible. It was practical for me to travel there, and possible as well. And on top of that, jewellery was relatively compact which meant I could pack what I acquired into my suitcase, thus avoiding having to pay duty on it. So I started thinking about a trip to Pakistan – all I needed was a couple of thousand pounds as seed money and I'd buy enough jewellery to sell in Morocco and start my own small business.

I was seriously considering this when I received a worrying call from my wife. She said that Imran had had even more trouble than usual catching his breath and that the whites of his eyes had gone blue. She'd taken him to a new doctor who confirmed that there was something wrong with his heart: my wife sent me the X-rays so I could look at them. I spoke to the doctor on the phone and she told me Imran had a blocked artery. She had given him medication and said there was a possibility that the drugs would work, but if not he'd have to have surgery. I was devastated, pulled brutally back to the time of my father's death and being alone in my grief. I started crying and couldn't stop. Despite knowing that if I left the country, I'd ruin my chances of getting permission to stay and would never be able to come back, I had go home.

And so it was that, on 18 September 2001, I left England for the last time and headed for Morocco. I was pleased I had done so even though it was hard to see Imran struggling for every breath, his nose permanently blocked as if he was suffering from terrible flu. I felt so powerless. The only thing I could be sure would help was to provide financially for him and for the rest of the family. So I stayed in Tangier until I managed to secure a business visa from the Pakistani consulate and then I set off.

I landed in Islamabad on 27 September 2001. I was still in the grip of my upset about Imran and, quite honestly, had no idea how I was to go about setting up my business. I started to scout the silver markets but didn't get far.

Still, I liked the country. I was staying in a place a taxi driver had taken me to when I first got there. It wasn't a hotel but a double room in a villa with its own shower and a kitchen downstairs. Although I didn't know the place, travelling on my own was something I was accustomed to. Some evenings I'd visit the Shah Faisal Mosque next to the villa. I was on the lookout for a good local person to guide me to the best place for silver and I managed to start a conversation with two guys who agreed to take me round the silver market so I could get a feel for what was on offer.

I'd only been in the country a few days when it became clear that the bombing of Afghanistan was about to begin. I'd watched the build-up on the TV in my room. The coverage was different from what I'd been used to in England because in Pakistan there was a lot more sympathy for ordinary Afghans. As I sat in my room worrying about my sick son, all I saw were images of fleeing refugees and all I could hear was people talking about the human catastrophe that would result from the American campaign.

If, instead of its indiscriminate bombardment, the US army had gone into the country to look for bin Laden and al-Qaeda, or even the Taliban for that matter, I'd have been in favour. But I didn't think, and still don't think, they had a right to bomb civilians from the air. You have only to put yourself in the shoes of the Afghan people to understand why. You can't selectively bomb a thousand people (was bin Laden's army any stronger than that?) who live among 29 million. You can't terrorise 29 million people and claim you are fighting terrorism. Afghanistan was a poor country: nobody spoke up for the people there. If they'd sent in ground troops, children and innocent men and women wouldn't have been so easily harmed.

In my room I watched heart-rending images, of women, children and old folk escaping the coming war. Consumed as I was by worry for my son, and alone in a strange country, it felt as if these people were sharing my misery and I theirs. I was pulled in by the children's cries, magnetised by them, and I found comfort in that pull because it distracted me from my own problems. The continuous stream of disturbing images had such an effect that my attention began to drift away from the silver markets and away, also, from Imran's ill health. Instead I grew increasingly obsessed with the idea that I should help alleviate the misery of these refugees whose eyes were so full of sorrow. This brought me relief from my own concerns: when I thought of helping others, I felt rested and in peace. The conviction grew in me that if I aided these people in their time of hardship then Allah would aid me and cure Imran of an illness I couldn't myself treat. It's possible that I was looking for an escape from Imran's plight, but at the time this didn't occur to me. Instead I threw myself into action. I asked the two guides who were supposed to be showing me the markets if there was a way of getting into Afghanistan. They told me of places on the border where I could cross without being detected.

I reckoned I could afford to commit up to ten days to helping the refugees before returning to Islamabad and continuing with my business plan. Once I'd decided to go, my heart almost flew with joy. Any trepidation I allayed by concentrating on the good I was going to do. I was determined to carry this through. I paid for a lift in a van filled with people going to Peshawar, a valley town near the Khyber Pass, which was about a two-hour drive away. I was aiming for Torkham because the two guys I'd met in Islamabad had told me that it was on the frontier of the two countries and that I'd be able to cross there.

Later when I was imprisoned in Kandahar I was astonished to hear the other prisoners talking about a Moroccan who'd used the most dangerous crossing, at Torkham, to get into Afghanistan. That must have been me: how strange it was to hear that everybody had assumed that, because that crossing was so unsafe, I must have been a British spy who was protected by the authorities or else I wouldn't have dared use it.

I wasn't a spy. I was a stranger, driven by an impulse I couldn't control but at the same time ignorant of the conditions both in Afghanistan and Pakistan. In Peshawar, I hailed a taxi and told the driver to take me to Torkham. I was wearing my European clothes and carrying a bag. We hadn't got far before we were stopped at a police checkpoint. The police took me to a tent and then, having asked for my passport, they asked me where I was headed. I was so naive I actually told them I was going to Torkham. Because I had a business visa they didn't arrest me but they told me that travel to Torkham was forbidden and that I'd have to go back to where I'd come from.

I caught a rickshaw to the busy market centre in Peshawar. I was still in an excited state and determined to achieve my mission.

True, I'd been nervous when the police stopped me; I was worried that they might arrest me – I knew that sort of thing happened in countries like Pakistan – and I didn't want to risk being pulled up again. Realising that my first mistake had been to travel in my usual European clothes, I bought Pakistani clothing – the traditional long shirt and loose trousers – and put them on. After that a smart-looking, suited, confident man must have spotted my confusion among the crowds and swirling dust and he asked me whether he could help. When I told him I wanted to go to Torkham but that the police had stopped me, he took me over to a car where there were two young men, neither of whom looked much older than twenty-one. The man with me asked them how much they'd charge to take me to Torkham.

At that point I no longer cared how much it was going to cost. I was far more concerned about the risks of being caught and possibly imprisoned. If that happened, how was I going to look after my family? Despite the men, whom I took to be experienced border crossers, telling me not to worry, I was almost engulfed by fear. But they were waiting for me: the time had come for a decision. I told them I still wanted to go and climbed into their car and, in my Pakistani disguise, obeyed their instruction to use my left hand to shade my face, hiding it from the policemen we passed. As we neared the checkpoint, I prayed I wouldn't be spotted. And so it came to pass: the police waved us through without even looking at me. I thanked Allah as we carried on. We came to a second checkpoint where once again I hid my face and this way we passed a further three or four checkpoints. I couldn't help noticing lines of trucks and buses full to overflowing – even the roofs were crammed with people – travelling in the opposite direction, coming from Afghanistan and heading into Peshawar.

We reached Torkham just before sunset, stopping short of the border checkpoint. All there was to see were a few small houses surrounded by high mountains. My two drivers introduced me to one of the inhabitants who, they said, would guide me into Afghanistan and then, after I'd paid them, they drove away.

My new guide asked for my passport which surprised me but I showed it to him, and he said it was OK and then he took me inside his small, one-room house. The only seat was a bed on which we both sat for a while. He told me we could only cross later that night so I gave him money to buy food. The mountains were by now completely cast in darkness which added to my sense of their enormity. I sat and waited nervously for the man to come back.

When he did, he seemed to have changed his mind. He said the control at the border was now too tight and that crossing would be dangerous for both of us. I assumed that he'd gone to talk to whomever it was he usually bribed to let people through, and that he was trying to get more money from me. I felt trapped and urgently needed to get moving, but for that I needed a guide so I had to keep him on side. I set to work, arguing with the man, telling him he had to take me across and that if he did he'd earn himself some badly needed cash, and eventually I managed to change his mind. I was wearing Nike trainers and he made me swap them for some rubber Pakistani shoes and then, before we had eaten, we set off.

6

With my guide carrying my bag, we picked our way through a wide valley of stones. We were walking in a riverbed, surrounded by high, black mountains. I could hear the sound of soft conversation, of men shifting about, and I could see lights twinkling. I assumed these belonged to the Pakistani soldiers my guide had bribed. He seemed by then to have lost his edginess. He walked confidently, acting as if I was also a Pakistani who was crossing with him to buy something from the other side, and the guards let us through. We walked in silence side by side and after about ten minutes came to a main road. There were small shops lining the road and, as happens in those parts, all the shopkeepers were hanging about outside. To my surprise – I'd been expecting a much longer walk – my guide told me that we were now in Afghanistan. I paid him and he quickly departed.

I looked around and up at those towering, dark mountains, like giant creatures, and I experienced the onset of a strange terror. My heart, which had been so full of joy at the prospect of meeting the refugees, now began to beat more in anxiety than excitement. That effervescent desire I'd had to get there and help and which had propelled me forward, making me persuade someone who hadn't wanted to take me, evaporated. I was on my own and this frightened me. But I couldn't go back. I'd crossed illegally and my guide had gone. I felt so vulnerable.

When you imagine doing something you plan it out in your mind, but plans and dreams are not the same as reality. From the first minute in Afghanistan I had the strangest feeling that I had become a refugee.

I started to question myself. Why had I let myself be diverted from my business and my son, Imran? What had made me head into bombardment, destruction and trouble? Was I running away from my own depression or keeping my conscience busy with the troubles of others so as to avoid my own? Or instead, and this is what I hoped, was I responding to a call from the innocent whose homes had been torn to shreds, and who had been made into widows and orphans while the world ignored their pleas for deliverance?

As this last thought occurred to me, I felt my distress lift. My dignity and my human duty, I decided, lay in easing such suffering. I was filled with new determination. I had crossed borders and mountains to save lives and this was what I was going to do.

Except I had no idea how to go about it. For the first time it dawned on me that I knew almost nothing about Afghanistan. I'd heard of Kabul but that was it. Since I wanted to go to where most people would be, I decided I would go to Kabul.

Parked by the small row of six or seven shops was a yellow cab. I bought a Pepsi from one of the shopkeepers and asked the taxi driver to take me to Kabul. It was difficult communicating with him but somehow we managed with a combination of a few words and a lot of signing – helped by shopkeepers who joined in with gestures. The driver was surprised by my request and one of the shopkeepers helped me to understand that Kabul was actually quite far away, at least a seven-hour drive, and that it wasn't possible to get there in the dark. When I asked him which was the closest town, he said Jalalabad which, he seemed to be saying, was one and a half hours' drive away. Good, I decided, I'd go to Jalalabad.

We agreed a price and set off. Being on the move helped me feel less insecure about what I was doing and about my naivety in travelling to a war-torn country about which I knew nothing save for the name of its capital city. I was anyway concentrating on not banging against the taxi door as the car jolted across rutted paths – Afghanistan's roads had always been bad, and the bombing that was soon to follow would make them much worse.

After about half an hour we were stopped by a man wielding a gun who was accompanied by a group of children. He wasn't wearing a uniform but he spoke with authority. I gathered that he was asking the driver to give the children a lift – they were young, the oldest, a girl, looked to me to be about thirteen – and I could tell that the driver was trying to refuse. I jumped in, making it clear that I wanted the children to come with me and so they did. We drove them for about twenty minutes before dropping them off in a small settlement. The driver told me that the man had been from the Taliban. I didn't mind. I thought I'd helped save some children from the bombardment and that made me feel much better about my mission.

By the time I reached Jalalabad and found myself a hotel room the bombing had started there too. It hadn't yet reached the centre of town but I could hear the thud of bombs falling and feel how they shook the windows and, at night, I could watch tracer bullets arcing up into the sky. It was chaos. Many people were trying to flee and I didn't know what to do. It was as if I'd been dreaming and all of a sudden I'd awakened in a war zone in an unknown place.

Everybody was on the move and, like them, and like my premonition, I understood I really had become a refugee. I would have been in a much worse position if it hadn't been for a Tunisian stranger who took pity on me and invited me to stay with him. He'd managed to get his wife and children to safety in Pakistan and now he looked after me, providing me with food, shelter and advice. In the end he found a car which was prepared to give me a lift to Kabul.

There were three people in the car and they didn't trust me. I think their attitude was that if someone came to Afghanistan then they should have contacts and friends, and it was clear I had neither. Nobody spoke for the five and a half hours of an agonisingly slow journey over broken roads. At one stage a tyre burst and we changed it, also in silence.

By the time we reached Kabul the bombing had escalated. People were heading in all different directions, many of them going east towards Khost which is on the Pakistan–Afghanistan border. Bombs kept dropping, day and night. It was terrifying. It was also clear that the Taliban were about to be driven out of Kabul and there was a generalised fear of what was going to happen when the Americans and their Afghan allies, the Northern Alliance, took over. In that situation I could see how impracticable my intention was to stay and help the refugees, especially since half the country seemed to be trying to leave. I knew I too must get out – even in those early days there were rumours about the fate befalling non-Afghan Arabs who were caught by the Americans – but I consoled myself by thinking that I could still help cook for these poor people who'd been forced by circumstances to leave their homes. In among the cars and lorries that were heading out I found an already full pickup truck prepared to take me. Soon we had joined a long convoy of vehicles all travelling in the direction of Khost.

It was an arduous journey, very bumpy and extremely dusty. The convoy wasn't organised. It would head in a particular direction and then, at some point, some of the vehicles would peel off and take a different road. The rest of us, and we included Turks, Arabs, Azerbaijanis, Afghans and Pakistanis, would continue, stopping occasionally by different villages to rest and wash and cook and eat. That's where I was able to help. I was always the first to volunteer my services and because of my training the kitchen became my domain. Others would gather wood while I'd organise the cooking in pots on open fires. We weren't only feeding the people of the convoy: the villages we stopped by were so poor they were grateful for the food we willingly shared with them and which they took away in plastic bags, even the leftover rice that had stuck to the pot because this they could give to their goats and sheep.

Despite feeling useful, I was also constantly worrying about my family. Sometimes I'd think about how badly I'd let them down and that would depress me. But when that happened, I'd make myself recover by recognising the good I was doing and this helped me regain confidence. Even to this day, and despite everything I've since endured, I'm proud that I can tell my children, and that they'll be able to tell their grandchildren, that I went to the assistance of people who were in terrible need.

It wasn't easy. In the twenty-five days I spent in Afghanistan, I witnessed much destruction and killing. On one sunny morning, I heard the sound of an American F16 skim the skies. It dropped a missile – I saw it clearly. I hurried to the site of the explosion but was unprepared for the sight that greeted me. The missile had hit a bus full of civilians. The bus was so badly crushed it looked like a folded metal sandwich. Shoes and belongings had been thrown everywhere with the force of the blast and they lay among the torn limbs of men, women and children. To the front of the bus I saw a woman whose skull had been smashed in. I saw her brain and hair burning, sending smoke into the air together with the smell of death. I saw a child no older than thirteen whose lower leg had been horribly twisted. I saw bone sticking out, and blood dripping like water squeezed from a cloth. The boy was calling for help but I was in a state of shock. I started to shout and to cry. I wanted to help but I didn't know what to do. I went closer to him, looking at him in horror, then retreated crying. And then again I went to help but couldn't because he was so entangled in the wreckage that I couldn't get him out. A woman also squashed under the wreckage was calling out, '*Khuday, Khuday*,' My Lord, My Lord.

These are sights that time can never erase from the memory. And because the F16 had so cleanly hit its target, I'll also never be able to shake off the suspicion that the pilot had probably boasted of it to his central command who would have rejoiced as children, wives, husbands, fathers and mothers screamed.

On another occasion I had been in the centre of Kabul when a vehicle was hit. This time I managed to help carry away scattered limbs. They felt warm, as if they'd been taken out of an oven. And then, on yet another occasion, a mosque was bombed and about eighty worshippers were killed at evening prayer.

The terror and ugliness of violent death was such that I thought I'd never smile again. After these attacks coffins came rushing in from every direction so that people could secure for themselves a safe place within the graveyard. The bombardment was targeting homes, mosques, cars and buses everywhere. I wondered whether Afghanistan had become a designated place for target practice.

Not all my experiences were terrible. Along the road on our convoy stops, two of my regulars were an Afghani man and his young son. The father would stand a few steps away and send his son – who was about eight years old – to collect their food. The son would look at me without speaking and then, once I'd given him the food, he'd disappear. I never knew whether he wasn't able to speak or was just too shy. When I touched his hands, his skin was rough and cracked from the nights of bitter cold. I'd try and make him laugh but he never smiled, not once.

One day this boy came to me as usual but on this occasion he was holding something. He lifted his hands and I saw in them a handful of walnuts which he meant me to take. I thanked him but, because I thought he was more in need of those nuts than me, I told him to keep them. He was adamant. He lifted up his hands, again and again, beseeching me with his black eyes. Every time I tried to give them back he would insist I take them. Then I heard his father call to me and saw him shaking his head and I understood that he also wanted me to take the nuts. As I did so, I looked into the eyes of this child. One moment all I could see was the distress and fear of war, and in the next I saw his appreciation of the things that I was doing.

This handful of walnuts carried by a child seemed heavier and better to me than all the nuts carried by all the trees of the world put together. At last I felt the satisfaction and rightness of what I'd tried to do by coming to Afghanistan.

7

Across the mountains we progressed, a river of people that kept merging and separating until at last someone told me we'd crossed the border into the Warzistan region in north-west Pakistan. We could still see planes flying above us as we moved on slowly from one village to the next. My company kept changing. I'd go, say, for twenty kilometres, with one group in a truck or car, and then I'd find myself with different people in a different vehicle. I continued to do the cooking whenever we stopped. Rumours kept circulating, including one in particular that the Pakistani police were making money by handing over anybody who seemed foreign, and especially Arabs, to the Americans. Other rumours, and reports on the radio, said that the Americans were sending these people in warships to Cuba. That frightened me. Along winding roads I travelled, through valleys and over mountains, heading for Bannu which people said was a big place. There, I thought, I'd be safe and able to phone home.

Bannu did turn out to be bigger than the other villages, but it wasn't very big. I knew I should find somewhere bigger and safer from which I could begin my real journey home. I got a lift in a taxi with a group of other men who'd also come out of

Afghanistan and were making for Lahore. My whole being was concentrating on getting there and calling my family. I wanted to tell them I was safe and find out how they were. Then, I thought, my troubles would be over.

It was not to be. I was with four other passengers in a nine-seat Mitsubishi Pajero and the driver was going too fast. A woman crossed the road ahead of us – I saw her coming – and the car hit her, but then, instead of stopping, the driver accelerated. We were screaming at him to stop but despite tears running down his face he took no notice until eventually he had to pull up at a petrol station where there was a police checkpoint. I watched the driver and his mate getting out and I watched them talking to the police and I knew they were trying to bribe them. I could also see this wasn't working. I kept a careful eye as the driver and his friend began sauntering round the car. I had a feeling that they were going to make a break for it and sure enough they had soon disappeared from sight leaving us passengers in the car. A couple of minutes later two policemen got into the front and began to drive us away.

The five of us were strangers to each other, even though we'd all come from Afghanistan. There was Manae, originally from Saudi Arabia, an orphan who, when his marriage plans went awry, decided to travel. He was very young and as a Muslim his only option was to travel in Africa, which he didn't fancy, or Pakistan and Afghanistan which is what he had done. He, God bless him, ended up dying in Guantánamo. There was a second Saudi, also very young, who was among the first to be released from Guantánamo along with another of our companions, and also a fellow Moroccan, but I have forgotten their names. And then there was Adil who was a Uighar, a member of a persecuted Muslim minority in China, who'd been jailed and tortured there and so had left and gone to Afghanistan as a refugee.

We were being driven back to where we'd come from and we didn't know why. All the policemen would tell us was that we were going to a police station. I tried to get more from them – after all, the accident had had nothing to do with us – but they didn't say anything: perhaps they didn't speak much English. With all the rumours I'd heard I was beginning to suspect that something really bad, something I could never have predicted, might be about to happen. Fate had me in its grip: I felt as if my world had frozen. I didn't know what to do.

So much of this story is so painful, it hurts me to revisit it. And yet the knowledge that the world should know what was done in the name of fighting terror drives me on.

I was terrified that I'd end up in Cuba and worried about what my family was going to do without me. But something in me wouldn't stay passive. Despite my fear, when we stopped for a moment, I told one of my fellows who was sitting in front of me (I was on a rear seat) to open their door and jump out. He was too scared: he froze. The car started up again. I carefully slid open the window beside me and pushed out my hand and managed to get hold of the door handle. Slowly I began to slide it open. Since our driver and his companion didn't speak Arabic I was able to tell the others that the next time we stopped, they should open their door and run.

So when we next stopped Manae jumped from one side and the other Saudi managed to get out the other door, and they ran. The rest of us also piled out, me last. Because I'd only been in Afghanistan for a short while (surely, I thought, when the authorities heard this, they'd release me) I decided to help the others escape by taking my time. One of the policemen actually got hold of me but I managed to wrench myself free of his grip and soon was running through a big field of sugar cane. The cane was so high it hid me from view. I ran for a while and then, reasoning that my pursuers would think that I'd naturally continue along the line from which I'd first come, and also thinking that I needed to go back to the road so I could get a lift out of there, I did a U-turn.

What happened next makes me laugh now to think of it, although at the time it felt anything but funny. We'd made our escape just after our vehicle had come off a bridge that spanned a wide stretch of water and now, when I ran back, I found myself returned almost to the point from which I'd first begun to run. But now I saw there was a large gathering of people by the road along with policemen holding machine guns and when I appeared every last one of them turned in my direction to stare at me. Short of jumping in the lake there was nowhere for me to go. I started to walk slowly towards the policemen as if I was going to give myself up. I took three confident, calm steps forward, but my fourth was a step backwards before I turned and ran as fast I could back into the sugar cane. It was a waste of time. The crowd ran after me and when I got stuck in some sandy ground – and by now I was very tired – they caught me.

I had been the last to run and the first to be caught. I was taken to a concrete holding cell where an armed policeman slapped me around the face before handcuffing me. I was soon joined by the Pakistani driver and his companion: the driver kept apologising for what he'd done. The three of us were taken to first one and then to a second police station where police kept asking me who I was, where I was from and who I'd been with. I answered truthfully but that didn't interest them. They kept asking me about my involvement with a group called the Lashkar Tigers. I had no idea what they were talking about: only later did I discover that this was a Pakistani-based terrorist group actually called Lashkare Taiba or LET. But it didn't matter what I said or what I'd done: they just kept on insisting I was a member of the Tigers.

After about three hours I was joined by three of my companions (the other Moroccan was still missing) as well as by an Afghani bystander who'd seen our predicament and tried to tell the police that we were innocent: he and the driver and his mate were later let go.

Having been kept blindfolded in a truck for the night, we were then driven to an intelligence-services prison in Lahore. I was put in a cell which had a high ceiling and no bed – only rags on its concrete floor. For the first few days I was continually interrogated. Police would bring in chairs and, with me on the floor, bombard me with questions. They'd ask things like who I was, and what I'd seen in Afghanistan, and also about all sorts of different groups. I tried to make them understand that since I hadn't even known about the existence of Jalalabad before I went I could hardly be expected to know anything about any groups, but they weren't interested. After a few days, however, they must have realised how new I'd been to Afghanistan and they stopped interrogating me so often. I was left in my cell, twenty-four hours a day.

I'd never been in prison before. It was awful: each day felt like a month. I couldn't stop worrying about my family and especially about Imran. In the beginning I consoled myself by thinking that once the police realised I was telling the truth, they'd let me out, for how could they continue to hold a mere cook? But I was simultaneously assailed by doubt. Trapped in a cell with only my fellow prisoners to talk to through the bars, I experienced a cycle of hope and depression. On Mondays I'd think that surely this was the week when I'd be freed. That would keep me buoyant until Friday when, because of the coming weekend, I knew I wasn't going to be let out – so then I'd sink back into depression.

Food, which has always been a comfort to me, was scarce. The man who gave it out would give me an extra slice of bread at every evening meal. I'd save this in my coat pocket so I could eat it before I slept. I used this coat as a pillow and one night I woke to find a mouse searching my hair with its claws. I jumped: I hated mice. When I'd calmed down I realised that it was trying to get hold of the bread I'd forgotten to eat. I ate the bread and went back to sleep. But the mouse returned and stood insistently at my head. Three times I shooed it away and three times it returned. I was baffled at how I was going to deal with this Pakistani mouse which was showing such great courage. I sniffed my coat pocket and realised it still smelt of bread, enough to attract the mouse. I turned the pocket inside out so the mouse could see for itself that there was nothing left but the smell of bread and then I left the coat by the door and slept without a pillow, and unbothered by the mouse.

I had another victory in that prison, although this time my adversary was the officer in charge. I couldn't bear being locked up in my cell twenty-four/seven so I asked to speak to him. In Pakistan, people who can speak English are respected so they took me to him. I told the officer that it wasn't right to lock us prisoners in our cells twenty-four hours a day, seven days a week. I said that we had to have fresh air and sight of the sun. I was talking from a human-rights point of view, and because of my English and my time in London, he was prepared to listen to what I had to say.

While I was in his office I witnessed the enactment of a farce. A low-ranking man kept running in and out, trying to please his superior. At one point the officer punched the bell and this man rushed in carrying a silver plate on which was a single carrot. The officer, who was fat and bald and leaning back in his chair, ate this carrot while continuing to talk to me. It was such a ridiculous sight: even now when I think about it, it makes me laugh. But my visit was worth it because I managed to win an important concession: the officer said he'd let me out into the garden for two hours a day. Only me, he continued; I was not to tell the others. This I refused, saying that I wouldn't accept any privileges unless all five of us from Bannu (by now the other Moroccan had been caught) were given them. At first he said no, but I persisted, telling him he had to respect our rights, and in the end he did give in.

My first prison: my first success. It was the most marvellous feeling. Going down the long corridor, past the others' cells, I knew they would be let out at different times and that it was my doing. And so it was that even before I reached Guantánamo, I'd

48

learned how to stand up for myself and how to organise. Perhaps it had something to do with being a chef and working in kitchens where you have to know how to handle people and get them to work together. This ability to organise others, combined with a determination to fight for rights, is part of what helped me overcome my years of unjust imprisonment.

After about twenty-two days, an FBI team arrived to interrogate me and to take my fingerprints and picture. They said this was to make sure that I wasn't on their wanted list and that they'd check and get back to me. The Pakistanis told me this appraisal would take two or three days and so I waited for two, for three, and more days.

It was terrible. There was nothing we could do but talk to each other but there's a limit to what you can keep on saying in that situation. At one point we went on hunger strike as a way of protesting our continued incarceration. Most of us didn't last long – when you have nothing to do and nothing to look forward to food becomes very important – but Manae held out. They took him to the garden, tied his legs with rope, threw the rope over the branches of a tree and pulled it. When he was hanging upside down they beat his feet. They took me to the garden to act as interpreter and they brought all kinds of food to tempt him. Eventually he agreed to start eating again.

When the FBI team asked me questions, unlike the Pakistanis who interrogated us in our cells, they used a special room. When the guards came to take us there they'd put shackles on our feet and hands and hoods over our heads. The second time they came for me I refused the hood – I told them to put it on Musharraf because he had sold us to the Americans. I said I wasn't a criminal and that I wouldn't wear a hood. The Pakistanis might have forced me into it, but the FBI told them to let me come without. I'd been relatively quiet up until that point but this success made me louder and readier to express my anger.

The FBI had brought an Egyptian interpreter who tried to intimidate me by telling me to talk or else. I told the Americans to remove him. They didn't, but after that he stopped threatening me. The FBI asked me all sorts of questions. The usual – who I was, what I had been doing, who I knew – and they showed me photos of men, particularly one called Abu Zubeida who, it turned out, was one of their high-value prisoners in Guantánamo. I'd never heard of Abu Zubeida or any of the other men they mentioned.

After forty-seven days, the Pakistanis told me they were going to take me to my embassy which would help me get home. I believed them. I'd always hoped it would end like this. That's why I hadn't written to my family yet. I hadn't wanted to worry them unnecessarily. When my jailers told me I'd soon be free I was very happy.

But when I was taken out of the prison to find my fellow prisoners also waiting, I knew they couldn't all be going my way. The Pakistanis had lied. Furious, I tried to stop them handcuffing me. As a result, instead of handcuffing me from the front, they wrenched my hands back and handcuffed me from behind before throwing me into a pickup truck.

Hooded, we were driven for about an hour and a half to a police station. We were held in a room there, but not for long, although I remember it clearly because the police swore at us and threatened us. I don't know why: perhaps they were preparing us for the next stage of our journey.

Then we were taken to a dungeon. As I was led down a set of steep stairs, I could smell bleach and musk and no air. Unable to see where I was going, I thought I must be heading into a torture chamber. The room they put me in, with rings on the wall, two high and two low as if to crucify prisoners, seemed to confirm my suspicions. The only furniture was a thick mattress on which I flung myself, terrified by the thought of what was coming next. But I was soon able to talk to other prisoners through a gap under the door, and two prisoners who were new to me, one a Yemeni and one from Jordan, reassured me that my worst fears weren't going to be realised.

I spent the night there shackled and woke up enraged. I started shouting, demanding to know why they'd imprisoned me and I also insulted their president calling him a criminal. As I was shouting, I heard the sound of keys clinking and then my cell door opened. They put a hood on me again, and now I was scared I was going to be punished for my insults (everything feels so much scarier when you can't see). They walked me up the stairs and into a vehicle. I was convinced they were going to do something dreadful to me.

I felt someone beside me. I didn't know if it was a policeman so I held my tongue, but eventually I heard Manae asking if that was me next to him. I was so relieved. Since Manae hadn't been shouting but was also in the car with me, I reckoned they couldn't have put me in there for special punishment. And besides, when you are afraid and alone, a friendly voice and a connection to another human being can make all the difference. Still, when our car pulled out, neither of us knew what fate awaited us.

They took the seven of us who'd been in the dungeon to Islamabad airport where they kept us handcuffed and in leg irons and black hoods. That combination of confinement and sensory deprivation is designed to increase fear, which was hardly necessary as I was anyway trying to fight the suspicion that the rumours of prisoners being sent to Cuba were true and this was what was about to happen to me. It was the most terrible nightmare: all I could think of was how much I'd let down my family and my sick son who'd been waiting for my return.

After a while, a short Pakistani man lifted my hood and took a good look into my eyes. I was furious with him for handing an innocent like me over to the Americans. In that short moment before he lowered the hood again, I was able to catch a quick glimpse of the room we were in: I assumed it must be the diplomatic lounge or something similar, because it was quite splendid, with marble tables, leather sofas and big, bright paintings on the wall. I also saw a short man holding a small purse and, behind him, men dressed in civilian clothes aiming guns at us.

Of the two new additions to our group, it turned out that the Yemeni guy, who was called Karama, had gone to Afghanistan on a drugs holiday. He ended up in Guantánamo where, because he didn't practise our religion, he couldn't really socialise. In the years of his incarceration – it was decided he was not an enemy combatant and returned to Yemen in 2005 – he hardly had a single conversation.

At that moment in the airport we were all too scared to say a word. The unknown was pressing in, silencing me as well but not indefinitely. I decided to pull myself out of the darkness that was enveloping me and also to try and save the others drowning with me. So I began to recite some short chapters of the Koran, and as I did, with the help of God, the fear in me subsided. My heart rested and I came back to myself. I think my recitation also had the same effect on the others. So I recited some more. Nobody stopped me – it was as if the lounge had been emptied of the guards. Calm prevailed.

And then I heard American accents. One of them was talking to the short Pakistani officer. First the American told the Pakistani that this was his first visit to Islamabad. The Pakistani expressed his pleasure at meeting the American about whom his colleagues had spoken very highly. I heard the distinctive shuffling of banknotes, and also some numbers mentioned: five hundred, one, two, and other numbers. I realised that they were counting money: it seemed we were being bought and sold in the diplomatic lounge at Islamabad airport. When that was done, the soldiers started taking us out. I heard shouted orders to stay still and the clink of changing cuffs and then the successive dragging of leg shackles, a sound which soon grew fainter. This sequence was repeated until, eventually, my turn came.

This was the first encounter I'd ever had with an American soldier, and before I saw any of them, I smelt their plastic gloves as they lifted off the Pakistani hood, which was shaped like a big envelope, and replaced it with an American one, which, more like a hat, was thicker, tighter and warmer, making it a lot scarier. While they were doing this I saw that their uniform was a desert-camouflage one. They took off the Pakistani cuffs and chains and replaced them with American shackles. After they had finished shackling me they hauled me up from my seat before throwing me to the ground. Then they searched me in a very disrespectful manner. As I was lying on my stomach, they spun me round, pulling me north, east south and west. They wanted either to disorientate me or to make me so dizzy I wouldn't be able to resist. They then stood me up and, shouting at me not to speak, they pulled me from both sides, the soldier on my right much more aggressively and faster than the man on the left. In this crooked fashion, they pushed and pulled me out to the runway.

8

They shackled me so tightly while I was in the plane I felt like a small insect fallen into a spider's web. As the plane roared up into the air, my attempts to find a more comfortable position were met by orders to neither move nor speak. The restraints they'd used on me caused me so much pain that I was relieved when, an hour or two later, I felt the aircraft beginning to lose altitude.

We had arrived at the military base of Bagram in Afghanistan. They roped us together and pulled us along the runway. Hooded, I couldn't see anything, but I could hear soldiers cheering. Of all the words they called out I most clearly remember 'Taliban, Taliban' being sung over and over again. My Uighur companion was ahead of me in the line: he was a short man and, as we'd been instructed, I had my hands on his shoulders. As we shuffled forward, blows rained down on us. I heard one of the soldiers laughingly tell his friends to leave the short one to him because 'he is my share'. I understood that he was probably referring to my Uighar friend although I had no idea what the soldier intended.

I tried to feel the ground with my feet, still in those Pakistani shoes, for clues as to where we were heading. It was smooth at some points, stony at others. I was consumed by fear. I thought I was going to be killed. I tried to prepare myself by figuring out the direction from which the first shots would come.

They stopped us and made us lie down on a cold tarmac floor. The blast of aircraft engines blocked any awareness of what else was going on around us. I was beaten from every direction and could feel wind blowing – from the plane turbines I assumed – and at the same time liquid splashing me. I have no idea what the liquid was. I didn't even think to smell it, so convinced was I that I was about to meet my end.

They hauled us up. They were swearing so wildly I can't bring myself to repeat the words they used. I was disorientated – a puppet being shoved this way and that. At one point I bumped into someone and called out an apology in English. I hadn't meant to, it was a slip of the tongue, but one of the soldiers demanded to know who it was who could speak English. When I said it was me, I felt a soldier coming close. He asked if I was scared and when I said, yes, I was, he pulled at me, shifting my hood enough for me to see that we had been led into a building. They stopped beating me after that: my loose tongue had saved me.

When they took off my hood and cuffs I saw that I was surrounded by soldiers, some of whom were holding batons. They told me to strip and, when I hesitated, they cracked their batons on the ground shouting that, if I didn't strip, they'd remove my clothes by force. One of the soldiers said he was the camp doctor and he carefully checked me all over. The way he examined each section of my skin, and got someone to note down any scars, I assumed he was looking for old bullet wounds. He prised open my mouth and ran a small wooden stick along my gums which meant, I knew, that he was swabbing to get my DNA. After that I was told to put on blue overalls.

Inside a huge concrete hangar, which had been built by the Russians when they'd been in Afghanistan, were a series of cages made out of layers of rolled razor wire with concrete floors. It was about 2 a.m. when I was shoved into one of these cages whose sharp edges were designed to stop us going near them. I was joining some Afghan prisoners, many of whom had been there for a few days or, in some cases, a few weeks. There were seven of us in total and we could see through the wires to other cages. I fell into a deep sleep only to be awakened at around 4 a.m. by a nurse handing out medicine. I saw that my Uighar friend was now also with us and that he had a black eye, a bleeding forehead and a swollen nose: the soldier who'd claimed him as his 'share' had kicked him in the face with heavy boots. Each time I tried to find out how he was, I was ordered to stay quiet until at last my friend told me not to worry about him. It was anyway hard to hear what he was saying because of the noise of huge generators which, as I soon learned, served the triple purpose of generating electricity, drowning out the screams of torture victims, and filling the air with stale smoke.

They kept us Arabs shackled for nineteen days (the Afghans weren't made to wear shackles). Above us and along the hangar there ran a concrete balcony so we were also constantly watched. Bagram was a lawless place. Prisoners told me how they used to hear screaming and, although I was only beaten and not tortured in Bagram, when I was in Guantánamo I met one prisoner who told me that he'd been shackled by both wrists to a ceiling high enough make him stand on his toes. He was kept like this, screaming with pain, for eleven days – I looked at him and couldn't comprehend how he'd survived it. Later, when I came out of Guantánamo, I heard about two prisoners, Habibullah and Dilawar, who had both died in Bagram after being similarly hung up and then beaten. Dilawar's autopsy report said that he had been struck so hard and so often that his legs had become 'pulpified'.

We who survived slept shackled, prayed shackled, ate shackled and without spoons straight out of the plastic bags our food came in. We even relieved ourselves in shackles, our hands only freed when we needed to sit on the toilet. This toilet, half a barrel with two metal straps across it, troubled us because there was no privacy either from our fellow prisoners or from the constant scrutiny of soldiers. There aren't many people in the world who feel OK about going to the toilet in public but for Muslims whose religious duty it is to keep our private parts concealed, this is especially difficult. It presented me with my first test as to whether I dared stand out by asserting myself: I told them that we needed curtains. When they said that prison regulations forbade this, I told them that no law of humanity, or of religion, could allow the treatment of prisoners as animals. My fellow prisoners joined in and we won a small victory: they let us use a curtain as long as we didn't raise it above waist height and our hands were always visible. (Yes, visible. Don't even try to imagine if such a thing is possible).

We were surrounded at all times by soldiers who kept their guns trained on us. Shackled as we were, still we were not allowed to talk in case, they said, we were planning an escape or riot. They had taken away our freedom without telling us why – the interrogators kept asking the same stupid questions without ever explaining why they were asking them – and now they proposed taking everything else from us as well. Held as I was in an iron fist, what I learned in Bagram is that I couldn't stay silent. The fires of oppression wouldn't, I decided, melt my determination, even if the odds were so stacked against me that it was unlikely that I'd win. As far as I am concerned, there is no life without freedom, honour and humanity. That is why, when I finally got to Guantánamo, I was ready to keep standing up and speaking out for our rights.

There's an incident in my past that sustained me during my incarceration. It happened one sunny morning in London, after my father died and just before I got really ill. I was walking past a block of council houses, each of them identical with their small front gardens, most of which were beautifully tended. I was admiring the flowers and the plants when I came across a house which had no garden, only tarmac. I stood and I looked at the tar, swollen like a belly with a cracked surface. No life here, I thought, and then to my amazement I realised that I was wrong and that some blades of grass had managed to push through the cracks. The sight astonished me. I got down on my knees and looked more closely at this tender green grass. I picked and crushed one blade which was so fragile and yet had a life force strong enough to push through tarmac. This experience kept coming back to me during my imprisonment. I felt that I was that weed and the tarmac was my jailer and that it was my destiny to survive.

All of us who had come from the Pakistani prison were in the same cage. Next to us, in another cage, were a few Arabs and next to them there was a cage for Afghans only. There was one old Afghani in a cage of his own as a punishment because he would never respond to the soldiers' orders: the Americans didn't understand that he was mentally ill, and they refused to listen when we told them. Although we were not supposed to talk, we still managed to exchange information and even, on one occasion, to throw some extra food packages that we had been given by mistake into a nearby cage.

On the second or third day in Bagram, the seven from my cage were locked in a room while a soldier held a rifle at the ready to stop us making any sound. I heard movement outside and someone asking that the door be opened, and I heard someone else reply that the door was locked because the room was unsuitable for use. An hour went by before they moved us back to our cage when the three Arabs in the neighbouring cage told us that we'd just missed a Red Cross visit. After that, whenever we were moved to that locked room, we knew that the Red Cross must have come again, and that they would never learn of our existence.

Some of the soldiers were particularly harsh. One woman was so driven to dominate us that, out of the blue, she forbade us from using water for ablution before prayers. I explained that if she stopped us washing that was tantamount to stopping us praying because we couldn't do one without the other. To this she replied: 'Then don't pray.' She was speaking to me from behind the razor wire as she pointed her rifle at my face. I couldn't let that go. Choosing my words carefully, I told her that there was nothing she could do either to hurt or to break me. I was partly testing to see her response and when she flew into a rage, her face contorted with hate, it confirmed what I'd suspected – that she was weak. This suspicion was doubly confirmed when she called for help. Soldiers came hurrying with batons, including her superior, a tall man who asked me whether I'd really said that the soldiers had no power or capability to hurt me. When I said yes, he was also enraged. 'We'll show you.' He kept hitting the floor with his baton. 'We'll show you, I'll break your knees.' He ordered the soldiers to separate me from the other prisoners so he could prove that they did have the power to hurt me.

I hadn't expected that my words, chosen only to hurt the feelings of the soldier who had gone too far, would have such an effect. But now I knew that I was going to be badly beaten. I braced myself. But just as they were about to lay into me, I heard a loud noise. The ground began to shake, the hanger building to sway. It was an earthquake. The terrified soldiers dropped their batons and ran to save themselves. It was different for me: I didn't think of this earthquake, which I knew had the capacity to demolish buildings and kill people, as frightening. Instead I saw it as a saviour that had delivered me from being beaten up, and I thanked God for it.

I was interrogated almost every day. I'd be taken by three soldiers, one of them walking behind me with a bat, past a series of closed doors until we reached the one intended for me. I had a number of different interrogators. There were two sets of two British interrogators who introduced themselves as being from MI5 or MI6, and who seemed to have come on short trips, and also another British man who spoke perfect Arabic and was there constantly working with the Americans. These Brits were almost always accompanied by an American from the FBI (who introduced himself as such), CIA (who always wore a CIA eagle badge) or US Military Intelligence (who was always in uniform). When I told the British interrogators about the mistreatment we were all experiencing they would just shrug and say their hands were tied: that this was American territory and they therefore had no power to help us. Still, they kept on asking questions and they were always the same questions – the names of people I knew and what they looked like – over and over again. In the beginning I answered to the best of my ability because I still believed they were after the truth and I thought that if I was honest they'd soon realise I was innocent.

But no matter what I said, they carried on interrogating me. I tried to convince them that I was a good man who'd never harm anybody. I told them stories that illustrated what a good citizen I'd been in London. It didn't matter what I said: they weren't listening. Never could I, a keen cinema fan, have imagined that I'd meet such people in the flesh. Now it felt as if I'd stepped into the screen and become part of the action, although the intelligence they exhibited was much less than in any movie. Eventually I got so tired of their questions and so bored of repeating the same answers that when they asked me to describe someone I'd just say, 'He looked like an Arab,' so as to avoid having to go through it all again. That angered one interrogator who said, 'What does an Arab look like?' Later, however, remarking on my red beard, he said I didn't look like an Arab. This tickled me – I pointed out that he was the one who'd said all Arabs didn't look alike, and here he was stereotyping us all. I said this to embarrass him and I was pleased when I saw it had worked. He'd been made to look silly in front of his English colleagues. It was all I could do, really, to get under their skin and claim back some power.

At one point I told them that since they were so unhappy with what I'd said, why didn't they tell me what they thought of me?

My American interrogator that day replied that they believed me to be an intelligent man, manipulative, who told good stories. He then opened my file and let me read the typewritten summary at the bottom, which contained the assessment he'd just described. That worried me: it seemed to imply that they thought I was playing with them. But I didn't want them to see my anxiety. So I told him that he'd left out one of my talents which was that I was a good actor. It was a provocative thing to say and it earned me the result I'd anticipated: both interrogators, who were sitting side by side opposite me, turned to each other and said, 'He was acting all this time,' before saying to me and in unison: 'You were lying during all the interrogations.' My ploy had worked and I felt a great sense of victory. I told them not to be so quick to judge me and that I had another story to relate. I knew they'd pay close attention because they believed that everything we said – even jokes and unimportant comments – might contain leads. So I spun out a tale of the time I'd set up a *Candid Camera*-style prank on a friend in London. They listened attentively, as I knew they would, until the end when they realised that I'd just been wasting their time.

At the end of nineteen days we were transferred and the way they did this was brutal. We were still shackled when they made us kneel while they placed hoods over our heads. Then they tied our hands behind our backs with a cord that then looped around the crease of our elbows and onto the next man until we were all tied together. They could have achieved the same effect by looping the cord loosely but instead they tightened it so that it stopped the flow of blood to our hands. As we were already chained – we couldn't possibly have escaped – the cord must have been meant to cause us pain. Which it did. When they pulled us, it was agony: men screamed out. But we soon learned that should we slow down or stop, we'd inflict pain on the others who were roped to us. My suspicions were confirmed when I was forced to kneel and wait for the plane. I felt someone bending and bringing their head close to mine, and I heard a rough voice whispering: 'From now on, we'll dictate your water, your sleep and your shit, until in the end there'll be no life left to you.' The whisper came to an abrupt halt but it continued to haunt me, growing louder throughout my ordeal.

By now we all knew that we were on our way to Guantánamo but although I'd so far been fed nothing but lies, hope's a funny thing and I still held on to the hope that I could trust my interrogators when they told me that mine would only be a short stay.

9

But before we reached Guantánamo, we first had to survive the military base at Kandahar, which was like Bagram but even harsher. On arrival we were made to lie face-down on the runway in the cold – it was the middle of the night in March – for what felt like hours as soldiers shouting 'Are you the ones who came to fight us?' stamped with their military boots on our heads. I could hear dogs barking and then the soldiers came and cut off our clothes with scissors while we were lying there. They then dragged each man, now naked, away. I could hear them taking the others before my turn came. Inside a tent, they forced me into a chair and ripped off my hood. I saw the floor of the tent but I couldn't make out what it was made of because it was so covered in dark hair. I saw my friends hooded, and naked, and tied to chairs. I started crying, not for myself but for the humiliation of my friends. Then they began to shave my face.

The soldiers were having fun, happily taking photos of all the naked men, and smoking cigarettes. When they finished shaving me, they threw me to the ground and put blue prison clothes on me. They couldn't find shoes my size so they shoved on a pair that was too small before standing me up and re-hooding me. I was trying to keep my nerve under that black hood, telling myself that my ordeal must soon be over. They dragged me into an old hangar, threw me down on the sandy floor, and took off my hood and handcuffs. They tried to take off my leg irons as well but the irons were so tight they'd welded to my skin. So they left them on, telling me not to talk.

There were about twenty-four cells in Kandahar, set out in tents in the open with guard towers overlooking them. But because I'd protested in Bagram about the toilet facilities, I was first put in a punishment cage inside a hangar. I reached my small cage at dawn and could see about ten others – with one prisoner in each. The prisoners were walking about in their small enclosures. Some of them looked at me but none of them said anything. With my leg irons still on I prayed and then, finding a blanket in the cell, I lay myself down.

I was woken by soldiers shouting '590' – this was the number I'd been given just before leaving Bagram – 'stand up, stand up.' There were three of them, all Americans, and I guessed they already knew I could speak English, although sometimes they used to yell in the same way at people who couldn't. They had brought saws to cut off my leg irons but the irons were by now so firmly embedded in my skin that they just ended up cutting into my flesh. When they saw the blood pooling they went away, soon to return with a giant pair of pliers. They tried to use these on my leg irons but this caused me such terrible pain I started screaming. One of the soldiers was particularly brutal: every time I screamed he swore and told me to shut up. The pliers didn't work and so eventually they got tired of trying and went away, returning on numerous occasions but still without success. It was only in the evening that they managed to break the shackles and so get them off me. It was such a relief: I thanked Allah for it.

Despite the ban on talking, the other prisoners told me that we were in a special punishment section. I assumed I was there for having been labelled a troublemaker but even so I was treated better than one of my fellow detainees who was kept bound in chains. He was allowed neither to sleep nor to sit in the ten days I spent there. If he as much as sagged they shouted at him to stand and they also kept taking him away for interrogation. Later I learned he was from Syria, and was regarded by the authorities as a high-value prisoner.

On my first day a shackled prisoner, guarded by two weapon-wielding soldiers, came to empty the toilet bucket. Under the pretence of instructing me in the use of the bucket, he told me that I'd spend a few days inside the hangar before being taken to the tents outside. This is how my chapter in Kandahar began: with punishment even though I'd done nothing wrong. I guessed that they must have received instructions from the soldiers at Bagram to welcome me in this manner and I wondered whether the trouble they had had taking my leg irons off had been a ploy designed to make my suffering worse.

They started taking me for interrogations. First they'd hood me, then handcuff me from behind. I'd have one soldier on either side and they'd haul me up by each entwining an arm under and around my armpits and up my neck so their hands would end up pressing down on the back of my neck. That's how I'd have to walk, face pushed down, stumbling forward in tight shoes until we reached the interrogation tents that were made of white canvas. During the hours I spent there, my hands would be free as each interrogator asked me what he wanted in his own special style. One liked to put a pistol on the table, closer to me than to himself, where I could easily have grabbed it. As he questioned me, he would be watching for my reaction to the pistol. It held no meaning for me: I'd never as much as touched a pistol and wouldn't contemplate killing another human being. But despite their individual differences, the questions each interrogator asked – where I'd lived, and worked, where I'd had coffee, who I knew, which mosque I'd worshipped at – stayed monotonously the same. As for their accusations, they were extremely odd.

One of the things they told me was that they'd run my picture through their computer system and come up with proof that I'd been in Chechnya. They kept insisting on this despite the fact that I'd never been anywhere near Chechnya in my life.

After a week they let me out of the punishment cells and into the general prison population. I was so happy to be out: even though it was hot and very dusty in the day, my time in Bagram, which had felt like the longest of my life, had been spent closed off from the sun and so I was relieved to see it again.

Kandahar looked like a medieval campsite except that, because it was also used as a military airport for both Americans and NATO forces, we could see modern-day planes taking off. The rest was very primitive. Inside rolls of razor wire piled one on top of the other to make unpassable barriers were rectangular barracks with canvas roofs stretched between wooden pillars. They were open-sided so that soldiers could see in – the only cover was the roof. There was razor wire between each barracks and at the front were metal doors surrounded by the ubiquitous razor wire. Each barracks – I think there were about twenty-four of them – held about twenty men. Around the tents the ground was a mixture of hard sand and gravel. Here there were no cuffs or irons: just the blazing sun.

We slept inside the tent barracks, on a kind of cardboard. During the day we'd either stay in the tents or wander around in the enclosure that surrounded them, breathing in the endless dust. We'd exchange repetitive stories of how we'd been handed to the Americans by the Pakistanis and about our bad treatment. On one occasion we were made to watch as a Pakistani prisoner was forced onto his knees with his hands on his head. This prisoner had kidney problems and he couldn't do it: he begged the soldiers for mercy but they just shouted at him to stay in that position. We watched and felt his pain but there was nothing we could do to help.

Each barracks had two buckets for use as a toilet. Every

morning, the soldiers would pick two prisoners who, now in legs irons, would have to walk through the tents, collecting the buckets and emptying them into a waste hole outside. I was allocated this duty on more than one occasion. It was an awful job, collecting waste at gunpoint but, once picked for the task, we'd carry it through with great aplomb. It gave us a chance to hear news of newcomers and interrogations, so that when we got back we could tell the others.

The soldiers would patrol the tents regularly. Their rules prohibited talking between more than three prisoners. If they saw four of us talking they'd punish us by making us kneel on the gravel for fifteen minutes with our hands on our heads. They would also make us do this when we hadn't broken any rules. They never bothered talking to us: they just shouted at the tops of their voices, cursing at us as a way of intimidating us. When they came to get one of us out they'd stand by the wire and order us to the back of the tent. We'd have to hurry there and kneel, hands on heads, like animals. Once they were satisfied that we were safely down, and covered by their machine guns, they'd call out a number. That prisoner would then get up and go to the front and stretch himself out, face down. The door would be opened to admit three running soldiers, two of whom would fall to their knees on the prone prisoner – sometimes they fell with enough force to crack ribs – and then the prisoner would have to put his feet up in the air and his hands behind his back to be shackled before being pulled up like a package and carried out by his armpits.

They did feed us but the quality of food varied greatly. Some days our food bags held pasta or lentils, or rice with pieces of chicken, served cold and, as at Bagram, without spoons. Sometimes the meals would come with a cookie, and sometimes a small box of raisins, but there was never enough to satisfy our hunger. At lunch they'd give us only Afghan bread. Once they failed to distribute any food at all to some of the prisoners, but when we told them this, they didn't believe us. When I asked if it wasn't possible that we could sometimes be right and they wrong, it infuriated them so much that they ordered me down on my knees on the gravel for thirty minutes. I heard one of them saying: 'We've found the brave one,' and after this, the soldiers would often make me kneel for fifteen minutes, and sometimes thirty, for no reason whatsoever. This could happen many times a day and at any time of the day. At first it was almost bearable, but before long the pain in my knees began to intensify. Knowing that tears would make no difference, I cut up some spare clothing given to me by kind prisoners and wrapped the pieces around my knees, under my trousers and out of sight, and this eased my pain during this particular punishment which went on for weeks.

There was much to complain about. The soldiers continued to use insults, intimidation and attacks against us. Sometimes a task force of twenty would surround the barracks in the middle of the night shouting, 'Get up, get up quickly,' as if fire had broken out. When, terrified and disorientated (this was usually between two and five), we did get up, they'd order us to kneel with our hands on our heads. Then they'd storm the tent, and seize us, one by one, twisting our hands back before throwing us to the ground and searching us. Any sound during such a search was deemed to be a signal to rise up, which would make them even more vicious. As this was happening, prisoners in nearby tents would be praying that they wouldn't be next because, once the soldiers had finished with one tent, they'd randomly pick another. During the attacks they also used dogs, blared out music from the loudspeakers and shone searchlights on us. The songs they played at full pelt were curse-laden, and this music, along with the sight of the soldiers in their black armour and black helmets, lent the scene a theatrical air, an impression which was reinforced by their insistence on videoing the mayhem.

Sometimes they even chose to terrify us this way during our early-morning Fajr prayer, while we were prostrated with our heads touching the ground. They'd always wait until we were deep in prayer before coming in to beat us. Once, one of the soldiers tried to lift me up while I was praying and when I refused to stand he dragged me by the neck so violently that my clothes tore. But worse than this was the fact that we were not allowed to use water to wash our hands or faces, or any other part of our bodies, either for prayer or for general hygiene. We would occasionally pour water from our drinking bottles over us – we'd do this, concealed behind our fellows, as a soldier moved between tents. If the soldiers caught us washing, we'd be subjected to fifteen minutes' kneeling: for prayers we had to resort to dry ablution, using the ground and stones to cleanse ourselves as we are allowed to if there is no water available. As a result of my months in Kandahar without a proper wash or change of clothes, I developed a skin rash on my head.

We were counted once a day at noon. We would line up in front of our tents and raise our hands when our numbers were called before turning so that the officer could see that this was the number written on our backs. This officer, whom we nicknamed Rambo, was famous for his arrogance. He'd make all the prisoners in the different tents line up outside in the sun awaiting their turn to be counted. Should a prisoner be late, he'd be punished. Except once when, in response to a late prisoner, the officer ordered everyone else to kneel for fifteen minutes. When the kneeling was over, the officer called on me to act as translator. He told me to tell the other prisoners that he'd excluded the late prisoner from punishment so that we'd all understand that this man had been the cause of our misery. It was clear the officer was trying to create a rift between us, so when I rejoined my companions I didn't relay anything he'd told me.

Just as in Bagram, our open bucket toilets were used to humiliate us. If someone was using the toilet when the time

69

came to call the numbers, that was no excuse; and if someone due for interrogation was found on the toilet, they wouldn't wait for him but would shout at him to get off and immediately lie on the ground. Thus did our captors try and sow terror in our hearts. They also played horrible games with us. Sometimes, in the evening, they'd order us to carry toilet buckets around the tent. Once they called on me to tell four prisoners to carry the buckets, in quick succession, and in circles, around our tent. This was a great humiliation for my comrades but I felt it was even more humiliating for me because I was having to translate the orders into Arabic and watch them being carried out. When the soldiers told me that, as translator, I wouldn't have to carry any buckets, I shouted at the top of my voice that I wanted to take part. When they told me to stop shouting, I picked up a bucket and began running. Round and round in circles I went, as they'd made the others do, shouting at the top of my voice as if I'd lost my mind. In fact, I almost did lose my mind, being degraded in this manner. However, after that, they didn't try to make us 'play' that particular game again.

Sometimes there were unexpected surprises. Once, for example, my interrogator presented me with a table laid out with food fit for a soldier. There was hot steak with gravy and mashed potatoes, and, to finish, a big chunk of chocolate fudge, and even as I ate it I couldn't stop salivating: I'd tasted nothing even half as sweet for more than four months. And after I'd finished the interrogator himself – he was a high-ranking one, almost a judge I think – prepared me some hot Chinese tea on the gas cylinder he'd had brought in, and in exchange I answered all his questions. He promised me a similar meal the following day but didn't deliver. I guess the intelligence I'd provided was not worth a soldier's dinner table.

The Red Cross also visited us in Kandahar. Once, when they asked me if I wanted to send a message to a relative, I didn't think my family knew where I was and I couldn't bear to tell them in a letter. I guess, even then, I was still hoping that I was going to be let out. So I asked if I could instead send a message to a friend in London. The Red Cross said I couldn't and then, after they'd gone, my interrogator wanted to know all about my friend in London. I didn't know how he knew of him, so I thought the Red Cross must have told him. Certainly we were constantly complaining to the Red Cross of our mistreatment, but nothing changed.

I was in Kandahar for almost three months. Then at last came the day for us to be moved. My interrogator told me to expect a distant place on the sea where I'd be given Arabic bread and good food. He didn't name Guantánamo but he didn't need to. He also told me I'd be asked questions there, but that I'd only be staying three months after which they'd give me five hundred dollars and a bus ticket so I could get back to my country and my family. He assured me that I was among those who wouldn't stay long.

We were taken off in groups of eight to be shaved, tied to each other with those cords that bound and pressed against our veins. Once again it was very painful and it was made worse by the way they kept pulling the cord. I heard a soldier who, indicating a Yemeni prisoner's thick eyebrows, said that these, too, needed shaving. Hearing this, and the rest of their terrible verbal abuse, I found myself wishing that I'd never learned their language.

Their barber did what he wanted with our hair, beards and eyebrows. Sometimes he shaved half a head or a cross into the head or bits of beards, all of which left us looking disfigured. This time he shaved off one of the Yemeni's eyebrows and half of the other. And all the while laughing soldiers took photographs.

When the barber had done with us, we were each given a three-quarters-full bucket of warm water and some soap and told to remove our clothes. As I stood there in my shorts, a soldier put his pistol to my face and told me that if I didn't take off all my clothes he would blow my head off. I wished then that the day for washing and shaving would never return.

Then they started to move us out. I was in the second-to-last group. At about 1 p.m. soldiers hauling chains and shackles on their shoulders arrived. We were made to kneel, hands on heads, at one end of the tent, but as soon as our number was called out we had to lie on the floor to be hooded. Then they dragged groups of seventeen of us, tied together by the cords, forward before making us kneel again. Since I'd learned we were to be moved, I had discarded the spare strips of cloth around my knees and as a result I was in severe pain. When I complained, a soldier punched me in the face, punch after punch, as a way of bidding me farewell. He hit me so hard, I knew my hood would tell the tale of what had happened to me to the man who was to wear it next.

We waited in a large tent, already extremely tired even though our journey hadn't yet begun. They replaced our hoods with goggles with blacked-out lenses, covered our ears with huge earmuffs, and strapped respirator muzzles across our faces which made breathing difficult. Before we boarded they sat us on the runway. I could hear the faint sound of clicks and see, through the gap in the goggles, flashes going off: the soldiers were taking more pictures. Then at last we were on a plane and arriving at another airport and boarding a second plane.

We were treated worse than animals. Not only were our hands shackled and our legs in irons but we also had chains around our waists, and all of these restraints were attached to a metal ring on the floor beneath our seats. And then there were the long cords hooking us together as well as all the paraphernalia they'd already put on us which was supposed to make us easier to handle but whose main purpose, I suspected, was to further infect us with fear. All sound was dulled and our eyes, which we rely on to warn us of danger, no longer functioned. Try it: muffle and blindfold yourself in the security of your home, and see how long it takes you to feel really uncomfortable. And then imagine what it was like to be kept this way for more than twenty-four hours. If crocodiles had been handled like this, animal rights organisations would have condemned it. But we were in the hands of a powerful military regime and we were going to a place where the law did not apply.

10

Despite everything I'd learned, part of me still hoped that my interrogator had been speaking the truth when he promised me that Guantánamo would be my first step home. But as soon as I reached the military base on the Cuban island, I understood that all my time in Pakistan, Bagram and Kandahar had only been a short stay in the neck of the bottle, and that I was now going to be forced right in.

After landing, we were made to kneel, where I mercifully cut short my agony by collapsing. They rushed me, half-conscious and on a stretcher, to a makeshift building which I later understood to be the clinic. When at last I had my goggles removed I blinked into the light, seeing many strangers, some of whom were in civilian clothes, while others were dressed like soldiers. Despite the fact that I'd no strength left, the doctor seemed more interested in cataloguing the state of my skin – he was looking for old scars or new wounds – than in checking me out physically. Having found nothing to indicate I'd ever been a fighter, he pronounced me well. I was ordered to wash under the clinic's small shower and after that was issued with my orange suit. Then, despite having travelled for twenty-six hours, I was taken straight for interrogation.

Military intelligence, the CIA and a translator were all waiting for me. The CIA always brought two or three interrogators, one to listen and the others to ask questions. The first question they asked me was whether I'd ever been arrested in the United States. Since I'd never even visited the US it was a ridiculous question, and I told them so. After that they asked whether I'd had prior knowledge of the 11 September attacks, whether I knew any of the perpetrators, and whether I'd ever seen or met Osama bin Laden. I couldn't understand why they were asking me, but later I learned that these were the same first questions they threw at every new arrival. I was shocked at the questions, but I was so tired and ill I just wanted to get it over with.

During my imprisonment I was interrogated so many times, and by so many different people. The questions were always the same. They wanted to know who I knew in London, who I saw, where I went. They seemed to be fishing for information about London and they persisted even though I had soon told them everything I knew. So similar were they that the sessions and the interrogators have merged in my memory. But the thing I do remember from that first one at Guantánamo, which lasted more than two hours, was that a female interrogator told me that I had no rights because Guantánamo was beyond the jurisdiction of the courts. She said that if I didn't cooperate I was going to spend the rest of my life there. Since I'd done nothing, there was nothing I could tell them: so from that very first moment I knew I was trapped. They had me and they weren't going to let me go. I felt so angry at being a scapegoat for Bush's war on terror, and also terrified that I'd never see my family again. At the same time, even in those early days, I made myself a promise that I would survive.

The first thing you'd see on entering Guantánamo (if, that is, you weren't hooded) would be a huge wire fence and a gate and Guantánamo's ironic motto, 'Honor Bound to Defend Freedom'. After I had been taken from interrogation to my cell, and after

I had spent a few days there, I began to understand more of the layout of the place. There were three camps: Camps 1, 2 and 3. The entrance to each camp was similarly gained. First you'd walk through a big metal gate. You'd be fenced in by high green mesh with a roof of razor wire above and then you'd reach another gate where a guard with keys would be waiting. Once through that gate you'd find yourself in a long concrete alleyway. To left and right were cell blocks made from metal shipping containers, each with its own name. Military imagination must have gone into overdrive to name these blocks. In Camp 1, for example, the cell blocks on the left were called Alpha, Bravo, Charlie and Delta, and on the right, Fox, Golf, I forget the third, and India. India was Camp 1's punishment block. In Camps 2 and 3 they continued down the alphabet, including Kilo, Lima, Mike, November, Oscar, Papa, Romeo, Sierra, Tango, the punishment blocks being November and Oscar. There were also three interrogation blocks, Brown, Yellow and Gold, which contained sealed rooms. After I'd been in Guantánamo a while they added more camps, including the steel and cement of Camp 6, and the relatively comfortable Camp 4 (I was never to be housed there).

Inside each cell block when I arrived were forty-eight cells, twenty-four in a line on the left and twenty-four on the right, with a corridor between them. Each cell measured about nine by seven foot (some were bigger than others by a foot or two) and they were made out of a diamond-patterned metal mesh, save for the back walls which, being the walls of the container were solid metal in which a slit window had been cut, almost like a postbox, which could only be opened and closed from the outside. In times of trouble these windows would be closed, sealing us in entirely. Because the walls separating one cell from the next and the row of cells from the corridor were mesh, you could see your neighbour on either side and also the people directly opposite and the corridor where the guards were, but that was about all you could see. Breezes would bring in the sea's salty moistness, but only in one cell block did I ever glimpse even a tiny piece of its vast blueness.

Each cell had a metal sheet that served as a bed base on which a thin mattress lay. When I first got to Guantánamo this metal bed was suspended from the mesh wall. After the first year, when protests kept flaring and the soldiers had trouble pulling prisoners out from beneath the beds, the authorities lowered the beds and boxed them in to stop us hiding there. On the corner of the bed was a black arrow that pointed towards the Qibla (that is, in the direction of Mecca) along with an inscription telling us Mecca was twelve thousand kilometres away.

In addition to the bed there was a toilet, like a pit latrine but made from metal that was embedded in the floor beside the solid metal wall: it was open to the cell and so, because of the mesh wire, open also to the whole block. Beside this latrine was a low metal sink – it reached just to my knees. In the door which led to the corridor were two slots: one at waist level through which food was pushed, and through which a prisoner could also be handcuffed, and one at floor level through which a prisoner's legs could be shackled. And this metallic environment – the only thing non-metallic were the human beings – was to be my home for years.

My first cell was in Mike block, number 32. On that first day, after my interrogation, I beheld for the first time Guantánamo's endless blue sky across which the occasional giant white cloud floated. I went straight to sleep – I couldn't help it, I was so exhausted. When I woke, I began to get to know my fellow prisoners. They were a mixed lot: from Saudi Arabia, Yemen, Turkmenistan and Pakistan, as well as Afghanistan. Some of the foreigners had visited Afghanistan before 9/11, some had been refugees there. My nearest neighbours were from Morocco and Jordan, and the Jordanian had lived in Afghanistan for many years, travelling between Afghanistan and Pakistan to sell honey, while the Moroccan had visited Afghanistan before 9/11. Both men were released before me. All my neighbours were also relatively new to Guantánamo – they'd arrived three weeks before and told me that they'd been so scared some of them had vomited in the interrogation room.

We were all complete beginners. We didn't even realise that other blocks existed until we heard banging and shouting from outside our container. After that we worked out that if the prisoners at the end of a block, by the container wall, shouted loudly enough they could make themselves heard by the prisoners in the block next door. That was one of the methods we used to pass messages and news between blocks.

Daily life was utterly monotonous: the only thing to break up the time were the five daily prayers, three meals, interrogations, showers and exercise periods. We had no clocks and no calendars and, apart from the occasional refurbishments of the camp, and the various big protests that stick in my mind, little happened that might have helped me register the passing of time. And because I was so ready to join in, and organise protests, I was punished by hardly ever being permitted pen and paper in my cell: which meant I couldn't note down the days, the weeks or the months as they passed. Only festivals like Ramadan and Eid stood out from the rest of the year. It wasn't just me: we all had trouble with time. When we reminisced about things that had happened during our incarceration we would often argue about when they'd taken place, our main reference point being whether it had happened in the year of our first or second or third Ramadan.

At the start they took me to interrogations often, sometimes twice a day. But after I'd been there a while, they stopped questioning me so regularly and I would only be seen in times of protest or punishment, or when, with tedious regularity, new interrogators arrived. At which point these newcomers would ask me the same stupid questions – what I'd been doing in Afghanistan, what I'd done in London, what mosques I'd attended – all over again.

For the twice-weekly showers, interrogations or any other

movements, we'd first be shackled and handcuffed through the slits in the door. If we were being sent to interrogation or to the clinic, we'd have an escort of two who'd arrive hauling chains and shackles on their shoulders. They'd also bring a note, written in English, designating the reason for this escort. For interrogation, we'd be taken out of the block and put into a small vehicle in which we could be driven for a few minutes to the interrogation room. If it was a shower day we'd be taken out of our cells, always alone, and walked to the small concrete shower room where we were supposed to be finished in five minutes but we always made sure to stay longer. Then it was exercise which took place outside. I say outside but in fact, even though the exercise cage that adjoined the block was in the open air, it was still enclosed by green netting. You could at least see the sky through the nets but all you could do there was walk up and down.

When I first got to Guantánamo exercise was taken alone for twenty minutes; after a few years they stretched this to an hour and let two prisoners in together. All the time we were out there we were watched by a guard in a tower. At times during my long years of incarceration, I was too depressed even to walk. I'd sit in that cage with my head in my hands, or even, at the worst time, just lie there. At other times, when I was feeling more energetic, I'd run up and down the small space like an animal in a zoo.

The only other exercise to be had was by walking the three steps up my cell and the three steps down, something I used to do interminably. Other than that I would pass my time talking to the prisoners on either side – we talked about our religion, our families, the ridiculous things that the interrogators had said to us – or reading my Koran, or praying, or just lying on my back on my bed and thinking.

I thought constantly about my family and worried about them. About six months in, I got my first letter from them – one of my brothers took on the task of writing to me on behalf of the whole family – which was a great relief because I'd been worried about the way my long silence would impact on them and now at least I knew that they knew where I was. Later I was to learn that they'd also got hold of a lawyer for me – but that would take longer to discover.

The letters, which came only sporadically, were deeply frustrating because as much as two-thirds would be blacked out by the censor. I'd learn, for example, that Imran had gone to hospital, but I wouldn't know when that had been (all dates and times were blacked out on the grounds that they posed a threat to security and could be indications of conspiracy) and so I couldn't properly assess this news. I felt so bad I wasn't there with them.

But in time I lost heart in writing to my family. I'd been writing to them so as keep up their spirits. I'd made promises to them which at the time I'd honestly believed: that it would turn out all right, that I'd soon be freed and home with them. But after I'd stopped believing that, how could I write to them? What could I say? Not wanting to raise false hopes, I stopped writing altogether.

My family suffered badly for the decisions I took. I know this, but at the same time I have no regrets. Seeing with my own eyes the abuse taking place all around me, I came to understand that I was a witness to democracy being put into the deepest of comas. From the very first I knew it was my responsibility to let the world know what was happening.

Before they took us out of our cells for interrogations, showers, exercise or any other reason, our escorts would first search our Korans, often more than once – they were particularly paranoid about the Koran which is something I never understood. Later they were instructed not to touch them, so they'd implicate us in this search instead: making us stand by the door and leaf through our holy book, even getting us to turn it upside down and shake out the pages, until they were satisfied. What was the point of making us search a book? We didn't possess anything apart from the soap, toothpaste and toothbrushes they'd issued us with, so what did they expect to find? The only answer I can come up with was that the soldiers who were being trained in how to police maximum security prisons hadn't the slightest regard for our religion or our feelings. Worse than that, they knew how much we cared about our Korans and so showed this disrespect to intensify our feelings of humiliation.

They'd also search us, inspecting our hair and beards before ordering us to open our mouths as if they were dentists. Then they'd search our bodies, our clothes and our flips-flops: they'd twist the flip-flops this way and that – as if there could be anything hidden there – and then they'd run their hands along the underside of our bare feet. If I asked them what they were looking for, there'd be no reply. I think they performed these searches so that the barrier between them and us would stay artificially high: the very act of searching helped stoke their fear of us while also making them feel that they were in control.

I later learned that before these soldiers came to Guantánamo, they'd be taken to the ruins of the Twin Towers. This was the last memory of their country to be imprinted on their minds and as a result when they got to Guantánamo they were already consumed by hatred for us, and inculcated with the conviction that we were the worst of the worst, possibly even capable of producing weapons from the thin air of our cells. I could see this in the way the new arrivals trembled when they first took hold of one of us. But they weren't just scared: they were also intent on humiliating us. They'd search us before interrogation, and once we were back in our cells they'd search us again. We were searched before a walk or a wash and then afterwards as well. That feeling of those alien hands, daily probing my body and my clothes, insulted and subdued me. I looked for reasons and meaning but I couldn't find it: nothing they did made any sense.

The soldiers were bad but in some ways the interrogators were worse. They were the highest authorities in the camp: the soldiers, doctors, nurses, library and postal service were all under their orders. Should we complain about being deprived of post or pictures of our children, we'd be told to speak to our interrogators. Ditto if a blanket or book was taken away. Even medication would be withheld until we answered questions. Some of the prisoners with plastic limbs would have them taken away until they answered the interrogator's questions. I saw one Afghani prisoner who, having had his false calf taken away, was reissued with one that was too small. The doctors threatened to cut off part of his leg under his knee so this new false leg would fit: only if he answered his interrogator's questions would the correct false limb be returned.

Just as I had in Kandahar, in Guantánamo at first I held onto the hope that they'd let me go as soon as they realised I was innocent. But I was not given a return ticket or five hundred dollars to get me home as I'd been promised; instead I was subjected to the same questions, over and over again, for a period of more than five years, as dozens of interrogators came and went. When I'd been there long enough, I started to see new faces in the interrogation rooms (along with the soldiers, the interrogators changed every six months) and I would hear new cheery voices saying, 'Hi, my name's Jim. I am your new interrogator.' Or Steve. Or David. Or John. Since they never had anything different to ask, the only explanation that makes any sense to me was that we'd been incarcerated not to let them determine our guilt or innocence but so that they could train new interrogators. I started to believe that the giant prison of Guantánamo was actually a giant training camp, that I'd been kidnapped and was there to be used as fodder for interrogators who never changed their approach. They were obsessed, for example, about asking me about the mosques I'd attended in London – easy enough to answer but my replies never seemed to satisfy them. They also kept asking me about Abu Issa's group of Moroccan fighters. Not only had I not heard of Abu Issa, but when they told me the name of his group they called it by its initials and I had absolutely no idea what these initials stood for. Only when, some two years later, I met my lawyer, did he explain what they were talking about.

One after the other the interrogators pulled out the same box of tricks. If, because of the monotony of their questions, or the overextended period of interrogation, we refused to answer, they'd try and entice us with good food, or chocolates or books. If this didn't work, they used coercion, like sleep deprivation or exposure to extreme cold.

There was a chaplain from the American military responsible for religious matters who distributed prayer beads and prayer hats, copies of the Koran, and sometimes prayer mats and religious books. The arrows by our beds and the presence of the chaplain projected an image to the public (I'd hear journalists visiting even though I never saw one since they'd close the windows during these visits) that we had freedom to practise our religion. In truth, however, they used religion to extort and pressurise us, punishing us by depriving us of our holy book and sometimes even preventing prisoners from praying and chanting the Adhan – the call to prayer.

I came to understand that they had brought me to Guantánamo to exploit and subjugate me, and the more I realised this, the more emboldened I became. I thought of that fragile grass in London that had pushed through solid tarmac, and I resolved not only to survive like that weed, but also to find ways to resist and challenge my oppressors.

11

I'd been in Guantánamo only a month. My normal cell was bad enough but I'd heard that solitary was even worse. One of the soldiers had told me about it, describing it as a cold place where the sun never shone, a bad place which I should do my best to avoid. I made a promise to myself that I'd never go there. But this, as it turned out, was not in my power.

My first punishment came after the Red Cross visited and asked us whether we wanted to send a letter to our families. I criticised their silence over the mistreatment we'd faced in Bagram and in Kandahar and which we were now facing in Guantánamo. I told them that all that mattered to them were letters: it was as if they were a postal organisation. The discussion became heated and voices were raised. I was sentenced to three days in my cell without blankets.

Although I didn't want my circumstances to get any worse, I found I wasn't prepared to keep quiet in the face of our continual abuse. Just as I'd gone to Afghanistan because I couldn't close my eyes to the suffering of innocent women and children, so I couldn't keep my mouth shut about the injustices of Guantánamo. Which is how I ended up in solitary in a maximum-security unit.

It happened after three soldiers beat up one of our fellow prisoners in the recreation yard. The entire block, including me, protested, shouting and hammering on metal with fists and the flats of our open hands. When soldiers ran in to stop us, we splashed them with water and so they retreated. A captain came to see why we were behaving this way, and because I spoke English, I acted as spokesman. This was often to become my role, telling the person in charge what the prisoners wanted.

On this occasion the soldiers who'd been involved in beating our friend were evacuated from the block and so we ended our protest. But three days later these same soldiers reappeared and at first sight of them the block erupted. Back came the captain to negotiate with me. I told him that having them on the block was a provocation and they should be removed: he countered with something none of us would ever believe – that they'd already been punished for their actions. The prisoners kept telling me to tell the captain that if the solders remained on our block the protest would escalate.

I knew the prison administration would never allow us to dictate the choice of soldiers and so this was one battle we couldn't win. I also knew that my fellow prisoners were too angry to stop. So I told the captain what they'd asked me to tell him. He left for a while and then came back with an absolute refusal to give in to our demand. I'd known we were bound to lose the negotiation: both sides were too intransigent. So, without consulting my fellow prisoners, I told the captain he should immediately leave the block because the plan was to splash him and he should get out before we did. He thanked me and, in a great hurry, left. After he'd gone, I told the prisoners what had happened, and they were very pleased I'd scared a captain, showing him that we, too, had some power.

As a result of my participation in this action, I was sent to a punishment block. Unlike the regular cells which were separated from each other by see-through mesh, the walls of the cells in the punishment blocks were made of solid metal. Being in one of them was equivalent to being in a box: prisoners could see neither daylight nor darkness, and, at least when I first got there, harsh artificial lights blared down twenty-four hours a day. Above the usual sink there was a boxed-in exhaust with a fan inside: it was supposed to suck out the stale air, but when it was on it was so noisy that you could barely think. They'd switch it on when there was any commotion in the block so that we wouldn't be able to hear each other.

There were twenty-four cells in each punishment block, twelve on one side and twelve on the other, with a corridor in between. The cells were air-conditioned by units that were set to blow in air so cold you couldn't stand directly beneath it. If the exhaust wasn't roaring you could talk to other prisoners through gaps in the door but you couldn't see them. The cell doors did have window hatches the soldiers could open so as to look in, but only when they were doing this, or serving us with food, could we get a glimpse of other prisoners. Later they removed these hatches and put in glass through which they could look and then, at least, we could see the prisoner opposite.

Imprisonment in Guantánamo in the normal cells wasn't like the movies where prisoners habitually register the passing of the days by scratching marks on their walls. What these pretend prisoners are doing is clocking off the time until they're released. Not us: we didn't know whether we'd ever be let out, never mind when, and so there was no sense in starting a countdown to freedom. As a result, as time went on, I cared less and less about it except to note when the religious festivals should be celebrated.

It was different, though, in punishment: then you'd be sentenced for a certain number of days according to your supposed crime. You were kept in the punishment cell, usually being let out every thirty days to spend a day in an ordinary cell, until you'd served your time, which meant there was an end in sight, if only the end of this particular period of punishment. But how to know when this end was due? Part of the problem of being in punishment was that, without a watch or any natural light, we'd no way of assessing the passing of time. When I couldn't stand it, I'd ask the soldiers how much time I had left, and sometimes they'd tell me. But if I asked them the actual time they might reply with either 'it's day' or 'it's night'. Nothing more. The only real way of keeping track was to register each call to prayer as it came through the PA system: after five prayers you knew another day had gone by, but it soon became difficult to keep count.

After six days of my first time in punishment they moved me to another block, not in Camps 2 and 3 where I'd previously been, but to Golf block in Camp 1.

Each block in Camp 1 was divided from the next by a green fence and a rolled-up barrier of wire mesh that was about four metres high. The different blocks were close enough for the occupants of one to talk to the occupants of the neighbouring block, although this was forbidden. As I entered my new block, the occupants welcomed me with cheerful cries of 'Marhaba, marhaba' ('Welcome, welcome') and they sang for me – something they did for every newcomer. It was such a warm welcome, it brought tears to my eyes, as did the way that they all stood there in their orange suits to greet someone they didn't know.

In Guantánamo the military had all the power. They chose the conflicts and they decided when these conflicts started and when they ended. We prisoners could only react to what they did – other than that it seemed we were completely powerless. Even so, we were under such extreme strain that the situation was always very volatile, and should we act together, we could occasionally force through change. I understood this properly for the first time one day in Golf block when I was coming back from interrogation. As the guard opened the block door, my fellow prisoners once again started to chant and clap to welcome me. The guard on my left – I remember him as very tall – didn't know I could speak English and he used that American swear word motherf****rs to refer to my fellow prisoners. To Muslims this is hugely insulting, so when I told the other prisoners what the guard had said they were furious and they took action. As we walked down the corridor, they started splashing the soldiers – I was in the middle so I didn't get the full force of the water.

My cell was at the end of the corridor so the soldiers had to escort me all the way down. They put me in my cell and then the soldier who'd sworn realised that he'd now have to walk back – and without my protection. The guard asked me what he should do and I told him his only choice was to apologise which he agreed to do. I told the prisoners this and then, as he went down the corridor, he stopped at every cell saying how sorry he was, and nobody splashed him. It was funny though, because he was already quite wet and I enjoyed the sight of a sopping soldier having to apologise to every inmate of my block.

That was a victory but it was short-lived. Many of our protests against infringements, big and small, of the few rights that still remained to us, and also as time went on against our indefinite incarceration, were met by increased repression and punishment. Since I was among those prisoners who were constantly speaking out, I soon found myself ricocheting between the ordinary and punishment cells and, after a while, having to make my home in punishment blocks. In fact, I ended up spending so much time there that one episode blurs into the next. But I can clearly remember the moment when I first decided to take the lead.

It happened about six months into my incarceration. The general in charge of Guantánamo, a brute by the name of General Miller who was also in charge at Abu Ghraib when the terrible abuses of prisoners were exposed, had seen how, when one of our number was attacked, we were ready to defend him: if one was denied food, we would all refuse to eat, and if one was deprived of his blanket, we would also discard ours. This solidarity was our only source of power, and so General Miller targeted it by creating a new 'order of classes' whose purpose was to split the camp into four sections.

An Arabic interpreter came round to each block to tell us about this new order. Each class, he told us, would differ from the next in terms of entitlement to food and possessions. Prisoners in first class, for example, were permitted two blankets, a white sheet, soap, toothpaste, toothbrush and a towel. The less privileged second class qualified for the same comfort items as the first, save for one blanket and towel. Third was further deprived of the white sheet while the least privileged fourth class was only allowed a blanket and one thin rubber mat. Some of the differences may seem petty – for example, first class was allowed an empty plastic bottle with a screw-on lid while second class could have the bottle but not the lid – but given how destitute we all were, these minor differences could easily come to matter.

General Miller then further upped the ante by letting the soldiers take away some of our basic possessions if we were said to have disobeyed instructions or broken camp rules, only returning these if we promised to subjugate ourselves to the soldiers' orders and camp rules. In addition, he decreed that those in punishment should not have access to their Korans.

It was a clever plan and it did have the capacity to divide us. If you had as little as we did, a bottle top, which meant your water wouldn't spill, could seem precious. And also, if you had a bottle top and the person in the cell next to you didn't, you could feel superior. Or if you had salt and they didn't, well, you could begin to regard yourself as the better person. The general's class system was thus an attempt to create a hierarchy of privileges among the prisoners which would then stop us from acting collectively.

I was already in a punishment block when this new order was announced. Because they'd opened the door hatches for us to see the interpreter we prisoners could also see each other. I cared nothing for the stupid possessions that they were promising to let us have if we were 'good' but I cared a great deal about this obvious attempt at divide and rule. So I took the notice that was given to me and told my fellows that we should not accept it. Then I tore it up and threw the pieces at the translator, and because of the force of the air conditioning they blew away. I told the other prisoners that we should stay firm and not let the prison administration split us apart. I told them that the new order was a plot which we had to break. As a starting point I encouraged my fellow prisoners in the punishment block to give up their privileges, keeping only a thin mattress and one blanket, and many of them did so. A mattress and blanket were all we really needed and if we all had that we'd be equal in our misery and equal in our strength.

That wasn't all we were up against at this time, though. I was also very involved in another ongoing protest that concerned the Koran.

I've already described how the soldiers used to search our Korans. Some went even further: throwing our holy book about – one soldier even threw a Koran into the toilet. Although I didn't want to be punished, I took part in a protest against this degradation by beating the door of my cell. I knew that their doing this, along with their touching of our private parts and the lack of curtains in showers and toilets, was a way of exhausting our energies and diverting us from protesting against our detention without trial, but I couldn't let these invasions of our physical space go unchallenged. And so I beat my door along with everyone else. That's the thing about being in Guantánamo: there were always protests happening. Life was lived out to the sound of shouting and beating doors.

But even so, when I first got there, these protests tended to be reactive and spontaneous, and running underneath them there was an air of hopelessness: few of us felt we had any control over our destinies or any way of stopping the things that were done to us. The longer I was in Guantánamo the more convinced I became of the need to change that sense of powerlessness. I concentrated at first on trying to figure out how to stop the soldiers from treating our Korans with such disrespect. With the prisoners in the cells on either side of mine, I set in motion a discussion about how we might change things. As our conversation heated up it filtered down the line of cells until the whole block was involved. Everybody chipped in with different ideas. Some proposed we go on hunger strike, others wanted us to stop all cooperation with the interrogators. But then I came up with a different idea: I suggested we simply return our Korans to the library. If we did that, I reasoned, then the administration wouldn't be able to keep up their pretence of giving us full religious freedom and, at the same time, they'd also not be able to use our holy book as leverage against us.

I knew how hard it was for the other prisoners to contemplate giving up their Korans. It was hard for me as well. Mine was my dearest possession, my security in tribulation, the light which delivered me from the darkness of my distress, and the longer I was locked up, the more precious it became. I was kept in a tiny cell twenty-four hours a day. I had nothing to do and very little to think about. I could think about my family but, because I was so worried about them and particularly about Imran's health, thinking about them would end up filling me with grief. So, instead, I read my Koran and I felt safe. While I was reading it, I would concentrate only on what was written there – while I was reading, I could ignore the complex of wires and metal that caged me in – and this helped me go deeper into my religion. I'd become a blinkered horse, focusing only on the path directly before me. In this way, I began to derive increasing joy from my reading, and to understand the book more fully. I also talked with my fellow prisoners about the meaning of the verses – this was one of our main topics of conversation.

So it was difficult for me to contemplate giving up my Koran and I knew the other prisoners felt similarly. And yet most of the prisoners understood that my suggestion had less to do with depriving ourselves of our Korans and more to do with protecting our holy book from our jailers' insults as well as exposing their hypocrisy. And so we debated the idea and it finally won the day.

We wanted our protest to be camp-wide. Since the soldiers controlled every aspect of our lives, organising was hard – should they get wind of a protest, they'd immediately isolate the ringleaders – but we always did find a way. Not only could we shout between blocks but we also learned to use the prison administration's way of operating against them. At that time, after a prisoner had served his punishment in one of the three punishment blocks, he'd be released back into the general prison population but not to the block he'd originally come from. This meant that prisoners, and especially the most disobedient among us, were continually meeting new prisoners: and this is the way we spread word of our impending resistance.

Our strategy agreed, the prisoners in our block began to hand our Korans over to the chaplain and translators, asking for them to be sent to safety in Mecca. We were using Mecca as leverage: making the administration understand that reverence for the Koran was a concern for Muslims all over the world. It didn't take long for our action to spread. Those who were initially punished were able to spread the news of what we'd decided and more and more prisoners began asking that their Korans be collected. The administration announced an emergency rule that prevented the return of Korans by which we knew that our analysis of camp policy was accurate and that our strategy was working.

My interrogator summoned me to ask why we were doing this, and I told him. I also warned him that because the Koran distracted us from our confinement, should we be without it for an extended period, our patience would snap and there would be rebellion throughout the camp. My interrogator could see I was speaking the truth and the administration agreed to our demand to prohibit the searching of the Koran. But their actions came too late: the prisoners no longer trusted the administration and they started refusing to take their Korans back. We'd reached a deadlock that went on for weeks: the administration trying to return our Korans, our not taking them, some prisoners still with Korans, some without.

It was while this protest was going on that General Miller's class division came into effect, and this included the deprivation of the Koran for prisoners on punishment, which created a fresh and even louder protest.

The triggering factor was an infringement by some of the soldiers of their own rules. Because of the deadlock, quite often when a prisoner from a non-punishment block was sent to join us in punishment he'd arrive holding his Koran in his handcuffed hands. Since Korans were now not allowed in punishment the soldiers were supposed to call the chaplain or the interpreter to collect the Koran and keep it safe until the prisoner had served his term of punishment. But on one awful night the soldiers broke their own rules and began to use force to remove Korans from prisoners arriving in the punishment block India.

They had done this to every prisoner as he came in (we usually had five or six arrive in a twenty-four-hour period), and witnessing it we'd become increasingly furious. We started banging on the doors and shouting. The soldiers took no notice. So, in order to get under their skin, and demean them in the same way that they were demeaning us, one of the prisoners started shouting out the name of Osama bin Laden. All the prisoners took up the chant, 'Osama bin Laden, Osama bin Laden.' I joined in as well. It was very scary at first to shout like this, but that night the soldiers had thrown petrol on a fire and when we'd objected they'd continued to provoke us.

Our shouts enraged the soldiers. They wanted to take something from us but we had so little: in the end they could only demand that we give up our towels. We refused to comply and continued to taunt them. So they sent for an emergency reaction force (ERF) to storm our cells.

ERFs were made up of five or six soldiers wielding shields and wearing black protective clothing over their military uniforms as well as helmets and protector plates for their calves and thighs. This gear was designed not only to protect them but also to cast fear: their appearance was much more terrifying than any normal human figure. When they were ready to attack a prisoner in his cell they'd form a human train, the soldier at the front wielding the large shield, the kind riot police use, like a fat tube cut in half lengthways. The cell door would be opened, another soldier would spray a hot gas known as OC (oleoresin capsicum) spray into the prisoner's face, causing excruciating pain to eyes, skin and throat as well as choking the prisoner and making him collapse. Once the prisoner was on the ground, the other soldiers would rush in and beat him.

They used different methods for these beatings. Some would press as hard as they could on the soft point behind our ears. Some would lift our heads off the ground before smashing them down on the metal floor. Some would twist our fingers back hard enough to break them. And all the time they were doing this they'd be shouting, 'Do not resist, do not move,' even though by this point it was impossible to do either. They also filmed these attacks, telling us this was to 'ensure the safety of the prisoner', which was laughable given the damage they were doing. Afterwards they'd use the medical kit they had brought with them to staunch the bleeding, bruising and bone fractures they'd inflicted on us. The unconsciousness was harder to patch up. But before this first aid was applied, our hands and feet would be shackled from behind as we lay face down on the floor; they'd put our faces over the toilet.

Such attacks would characteristically last for about fifteen minutes and then, after administering the first aid, they'd remove the shackles and then, holding on to each other, would slowly withdraw from the cell in a line, the last soldier remaining to restrain the prisoner until he was finally pulled from the prisoner's body with such force that they'd all end up falling backwards. Then the cell door would be slammed shut.

And all the time other prisoners could see what was happening through gaps around the door hatches, although we weren't in a position to do anything other than bear witness and find ways to express our rage. We'd call to each other, beating on the doors and walls of their cells so the clatter of iron would reach the heart of our broken friend, and also the soldiers' ears, and in that way show that we prisoners were as one.

The ERF attacked prisoners one by one. It didn't bother them to have to face down one or even a handful of prisoners, but if the whole block resisted them they risked losing control. And that night in India these attacks were repeated at least twenty times. Our Saudi Arabian friend, Mishal, was unlucky to be the first victim of the ERF's brutality. And after that none of us was spared.

They had started in Mishal's cell. I could hear him yelling and I could hear the sounds of them beating him. Through the small gaps in the edges of the food slots in our doors, some of the prisoners saw them bringing Mishal out on a stretcher. They also saw blood on his towel. They started calling, 'We saw blood, we saw blood, we saw blood.'

The situation escalated. By now we were all yelling into the exhaust pipes at the back of our cells, because if we shouted there, other blocks might hear us. Mishal was taken to hospital but our night didn't end there. They began to beat us, cell by cell, while we resisted, refusing to give up our towels. The noise and panic was immense. It went on until 5 a.m. by which time other prisoners had also sustained injuries and been taken off to hospital.

These other injured prisoners were later returned to the blocks but Mishal didn't reappear. This meant he must have been seriously hurt. It was then our duty, as we saw it, to spread the news of what had happened to the other blocks and to ask them to help find out how Mishal was.

After such a long, noisy night other prisoners and other soldiers would have known that something terrifying had happened in India block. But even though the other blocks were only a few metres away, ours was so closed it was difficult to make contact. We needed to know whether Mishal was still alive. We asked the soldiers but they said it was none of our business. So we discussed our next move and I came up with the suggestion that we should accuse General Miller, as the man in charge, and the chaplain (because his agreement to the banning of the Koran in the punishment block had been central to what had happened) of murdering Mishal.

We called for an interpreter and asked him to inform the administration of our accusations. We didn't do this because we needed translation but because we knew that the interpreters talked to each other, and also to the soldiers, and so they'd all get to hear of our accusations. For this same reason we shouted to our neighbours in the adjacent block asking them to also inform their interpreters.

Three days later the administration broadcast some news on the PA – an unusual step for them. Although the call to prayer was played over the system five times a day it was only very rarely used for other notices. What the PA told us was that Mishal had tried to commit suicide, that only fast intervention by the soldiers had saved him and that he was now recovering in intensive care.

With this announcement Mishal's plight was out in the open. We knew he was alive, although we still didn't know how badly he'd been injured. We didn't for a moment believe the suicide story, not after some of us had seen the blood on his towel. Yet it was a victory of sorts. Despite our vulnerability we'd managed to put pressure not only on our low-ranking jailers, but also on the highest authority in Guantánamo: General Miller. We started to disuss how to capitalise on this.

This moment marked a turning point for me. I was rushed off to see my interrogator whom I found eagerly awaiting me. He asked me if I knew what my new nickname among the soldiers was. When I said no, he told me that it was 'the General'. I was sitting on a chair and shackled to an iron ring in the floor. He moved closer in his comfortable office chair, put his hands on my knees and looked me straight in the eyes. 'Get off the stage,' he said, 'now. You are under the spotlight, in an exposed position. If you don't step down you'll fall and get hurt.' He told me then that he'd been sent by the colonel, a senior-ranking officer, to deliver this message and that this was the last time I'd be told. From now on, he continued, I should consider myself warned and should take responsibility for my actions.

He made me feel like a powerful ringleader – something I'd not expected to be – and this shocked and scared me. I wasn't prepared for it and I didn't know what to do. But I pretended not to be scared, and told him that I wouldn't step down until they started respecting us and the Koran. He told me to get off the stage and they'd look into the matter of the Koran, and then he went away. I never saw him again.

Back at India block my companions were waiting to continue our discussions. I was still very shaken. I apologised and asked if we could adjourn the matter until the next day. I didn't tell them about the threat from the interrogator – I needed to think about what he'd said. I felt alone and in danger: it was no minor matter to be threatened by an interrogator who was acting as proxy for the colonel.

For the first time I realised that I was considered a threat by General Miller and his cronies. At the same time I was also a weak prisoner, shackled in the tight fist of an enormous army. I was right to be afraid. Yet I knew that if I told my friends about my fear, or shared any thoughts about withdrawing, this would make them afraid like me. If I stepped back they might also and then who would safeguard our Korans and protect us from further attacks?

I went round in circles all night, calling on Allah to make me steadfast and guide me. By morning my thoughts had cleared and my fear had evaporated. I told my companions what had happened between me and the interrogator and I also told them that we needed to keep on with our protests. Twenty minutes later I was taken away and put in Oscar, a punishment block where I was on my own with a guard of three soldiers keeping me under constant watch. I was kept there for five days. Meanwhile, back in India, the soldiers tried to make the protesting prisoners wear straitjackets intended for the mentally ill. The prisoners immediately started a hunger strike which forced the officials to back down and return their orange clothes.

My companions didn't forget me. They sent messages to other blocks telling them I was missing and, thus united, they put pressure on the camp officials to reveal my whereabouts. The administration gave in. They sent Omar Degayes from Libya, along with an escort of soldiers, to Oscar to show him that I was there and that I was fine.

I wasn't fine, though. I was taken to the interrogation room every night where I was intimidated. In between, I was subjected to sleep deprivation with the three soldiers shouting at me to wake up should my head as much as droop. Omar wouldn't have known this, of course, as he was only allowed to take one quick look through the window.

When I was returned to India block we decided to pile on the pressure. We kept up our accusation that they'd attacked Mishal and we kept on pointing the finger of blame at the general. Our persistence produced a variety of strange reactions from the administration. In a bid to imply that Mishal had tried to hang himself, they produced blankets specially designed (they were thicker and of much looser weave) to prevent them from being used in hanging. They also accused me of issuing a fatwa making suicide acceptable although they didn't specify where or when I was supposed to have done this. They also ignored the fact that fatwas are rulings about Islamic law that can only be issued by high-ranking scholars. But despite the lack of any evidence for this accusation – and despite the fact it made no sense – it was later to be added to the list of charges against me. And at the time when they made it, it really worried me because it showed that by trying to insist that Mishal had tried to kill himself on my instructions, they were intent on making me out to be something I wasn't and this, I knew, could be very dangerous for me.

Meanwhile, doubt had now begun to creep in about how Mishal was. I suggested we put more pressure on General Miller by getting our interpreter to tell him that we demanded his permission to carry out funeral prayers for Mishal. We asked that this be a collective service that could reach the whole camp by PA so that everybody could take part. Our real purpose was to get permission to visit Mishal in hospital and see his condition for ourselves.

The administration responded by saying that we had no right to visit him because this would be an intrusion on his privacy, as well as a breach of his confidential medical file. Our answer was to tell them that visiting the sick was our religious duty, and we had to abide by this even in captivity. To drive the message home further we wrote 'Allow us to pray the funeral service' with white toothpaste on our brown rubber mats. Then I suggested we refuse to return the plastic spoons that came with every meal. I proposed this because I'd noticed that the soldiers seemed actually to believe we could use the spoons as weapons and were always careful to get them back after every meal. It was agreed that we should all put our spoons through the mesh screen around the exhaust.

As soon as the soldiers realised that our spoons hadn't been returned with our plates, they rushed to our block. There were a whole lot of them – interrogators, camp officials and ordinary soldiers. It looked as if war had broken out – and all because of a few plastic spoons that were sitting peaceably behind a mesh screen. The interrogators, who'd been the ones to start the rumour that we were capable of using spoons as weapons, must have thought it had actually come to pass.

They stood by my cell door to ask about our refusal to return the spoons. I told my friends to lift their brown mats with their toothpaste writing. Seeing our request to pray for the dead Mishal, they said that we must first return the spoons before they'd talk to us about him. Then they shackled and handcuffed me and came into my cell to get my spoon. They couldn't find it. I told them where it was but they couldn't get it out because the openings in the mesh were too small. It was a bizarre scene – grown men scrabbling for a plastic spoon all because they'd believed the interrogators, men who, in our experience, were never bored with inventing their own reality and who in this case had created the possibility of dangerous plastic spoons. At first I thought it was funny, but I changed my mind when the ERF arrived to drag me to an interrogation room.

They attacked me there, pressing at the vulnerable point behind my ears and twisting my fingers and hands almost to breaking point. These were ordinary soldiers but they were acting under the watchful gaze of senior officials who crowded together behind the smoked glass. Then the chief interrogator came in and he was so furious that despite the fact that it was me who was chained to the ground and in pain, his, and not my, knees were trembling. He kept on asking: 'Why did you use the spoons? Why the spoons?' before telling the soldiers to stop messing with me so I could answer.

I gave him a nonsensical answer designed to fuel his rage. I told him that we'd noticed that they were obsessed with the spoons, so we'd decided that spoons must hold some special importance for them, which is why we hid them in a place where neither we nor they could get at them. He asked me what the point of our protest was. I told him we wanted to visit Mishal in the hospital and that we also wanted the soldiers to respect the Koran and to stop attacking us.

At this point a different officer, one I'd not previously met, came in and ordered that two seats – one made from iron and one from leather – be brought in. He told the soldiers to give me the comfortable leather seat while he took the iron one. He had two cigarettes, one of which he lit and the other of which he put on the ground. Then he did the oddest thing. While facing me, he spread one of his hands across his face until he was looking at me through his fingers. He moved this hand to left and right while saying: 'I can't see any jinns or angels with you.' I didn't know what he was talking about but he didn't care. 'You're on your own,' he said as he continued to jiggle the hand. 'You're weak. Other people have jinns and angels to protect them, but I can see you're alone.'

It was the most ridiculous spectacle I'd ever witnessed. He was acting as if he believed in black magic, and as if I did as well. I couldn't quite credit it that a grown man should choose to make such a fool of himself. I told him I didn't need spirits or angels. This made him furious. He ordered the guard to swap our chairs, so that he now had the leather one while I was on the iron one. 'I deserve this more than you,' he told me as he sat down again. Then he asked why I'd incited the protest and created dissent. 'The Lord doesn't like this,' he said. 'It's not good,' and continued, 'we are all God's children.'

I interrupted him. 'You're wrong,' I said. 'God doesn't have children. I am the son of my father and my mother.' That provoked him even further. He told the soldiers to remove my chair and sit me on the floor. After that he ordered them to stand me up. Finally he said: 'I'll make you drop your plans,' and then he left. When the doors opened briefly to let him out, I saw the other senior officials walking past as they vacated their positions behind the smoked glass.

It was clear to me that I was in trouble and that I kept getting into trouble because of my refusal to play their game. I also knew that if I gave in I'd have an easier time of it. There was something in me, however, that just wouldn't let them treat me like this, as if I wasn't a human being. Another example was when I was in punishment and my breakfast of scrambled egg, porridge and bread was delivered with the bread on top of the porridge so it had all gone soggy. I checked whether this was deliberate by asking the person in the adjacent cell whether his breakfast was the same and he confirmed it was, as was the man's in the cell next to his. The soldiers were playing one of their sadistic games with us. I told my fellow prisoners not to eat, and to pass this message along the block, and then I called the guard and asked him to fetch whoever was in charge. He promised he would but then he came back with another solider of exactly the same rank as him. There were four of them now, outside my cell, all of them playing with me. So I decided to play as well. I said I wanted to know why the bread was on the porridge and I held out my plate so they'd open the food hatch to look at it. As soon as they did, I shoved the plate hard at the closest soldier. My aim was perfect: if I'd practised a hundred times I might never have got it right – but this first and only time I got a bullseye, hitting him straight in the face. The plate stuck for a moment before slithering down, leaving his face all yellow and white. He looked so absurd even his fellow soldiers burst out laughing. This was a victory for me and an especially satisfying one because that particular soldier was famous for his viciousness. I knew that what I'd done would make him hate me more, but I also knew that showing this kind of resistance was the thing that kept me alive.

I wasn't alone in my resistance – many other prisoners also contributed ideas and took part in our campaigns and some, like Shaker who will feature more later, were at the forefront of this resistance. But the authorities had marked me as a ringleader, a position that had partly been thrust upon me because I spoke English, and when I began to suffer for it, I couldn't bring myself to back down. I had done nothing to deserve being locked up in Guantánamo. I was innocent. I deserved to have my family, my friends and my life back. In the face of their refusal to listen to me, I couldn't give in. I did it for myself and my actions repaid me. Without my determination to keep on protesting against the things they were doing to us, I'd have lost hope and, after that, my mind. And my resistance served another purpose as well: they'd taken away everything from me and I wanted them to feel their lack of power and their stupidity so that they could begin to understand what they were doing to us.

12

I soon began to understand what the officer had meant when he'd threatened me with the punishments that would be heaped on me if I didn't get off the stage. They took me to Brown block which was one of the three interrogation blocks. The room they put me in was small and sealed in. It was like being in a train carriage that had no windows. There was a chair next to an iron ring that was anchored to the floor. I was told to sit in the chair and then they shackled my feet to the ring. My hands were also shackled in front of me and the chain which held the shackles was then wrapped around my waist. A smoked window hid the faces of the observers watching me from outside and, in addition, high in one corner was a camera trained on the chair. Once they'd immobilised me in a chair, they reprogrammed the air-conditioning unit and left.

Alone in the stillness, I could hear nothing but the sound of cold air blowing. The temperature began to drop and I was soon shaking with cold. Knowing that they had to be watching me through the glass, I called out to complain. A soldier came in to tell me that he couldn't change the setting because it was programmed like that by order of the interrogator. He spoke to me in a completely normal voice, as if this was an everyday occurrence, and I knew that what they wanted was for me to beg them to fetch my interrogator because that would begin the process of me being dependent on him. I didn't ask for the interrogator and so the soldier left, closing the door behind him. The cold intensified, but it was no longer my only problem: the way they'd shackled me to the chair and then to the ground caused me pain in my back that soon became almost unbearable. Despite my protests, they kept me in there for over six hours. Nobody came to question me: they just left me there shivering and in agony until at last two soldiers entered, unlocked me from the chair and took me back to an ordinary cell.

I didn't know why they'd taken me back. Perhaps, I thought, they wanted me to tell the other prisoners what had been done to me so as to deter them from further protest or perhaps they were trying to make me believe my ordeal was over. It wasn't. Two hours later, they came again, taking me back to the interrogation room. They tied me into the chair, and whenever I tried to lean my head to left or right in an attempt to relieve the pain, a soldier would burst in holding a stick, like a broom handle, which he would bang on the floor while shouting, 'Don't sleep, don't sleep.' As if I could have slept in those conditions.

Apart from these incursions, I was totally isolated. I'd work out the time passing by counting small things, like the call to prayer, or the routine of breakfast or lunch, or when they collected the remains of meals, or occasionally if a soldier was kind enough to tell me when I asked. So on the second occasion, I knew that they'd kept me there for eight hours before taking me back to my cell where I threw myself onto my metal bed. I was exhausted and I needed sleep, but my mind was working so hard it wouldn't let up in the two hours which I feared were all I had.

I was right. Two hours later, back they came to drag me to the interrogation room again. This time the pain in my back and now my kidneys was unbearable. The chain around my waist was so tight that it stuck my hands to my belly and also made me bend in so that, with both feet also shackled, I sat on the chair in an inverted U-shape. Because the pain was so bad, I used my bent knees to topple myself onto the floor to try and relieve it. There I lay, still chained and curled like a foetus, as two soldiers rushed in, shouting, so loudly they frightened me, that sleep was forbidden. When I described the intensity of my pain, they told me to get back into the seat and that they'd call a nurse. When I complained about the cold, they repeated what they'd said the last time: that the rules didn't allow them to adjust the temperature without explicit permission from the interrogators.

The nurse arrived, questioned me about my pain, gave me some tablets and left. The tablets, which were only painkillers, didn't really help. I was then kept in that room for another eight hours before being returned to my cell. This, I'd begun to understand, was going to be my new routine: six- or eight-hour sessions in intense cold and pain during which I was prevented from sleeping, followed by two hours' break, in an endless cycle, twenty-four hours a day. When I heard the clanking of keys as the soldiers approached the interrogation room, I knew I was going to be allowed out and I'd eagerly await the sound of the keys turning in the lock. But if I happened to be in my cell when I heard a different kind of clanking – this time of shackles coming closer – I'd feel my panic rise as I faced the prospect of another long session. As a result I began to associate keys with the knowledge that I'd survive, while the clanking of chains filled me with dread.

By the second or third day, the hours began to blur into each other. I hurled myself onto the ground, this time refusing to get back up until they fetched the nurse. When he got there I told him that his tablets were useless and the pain was only alleviated when I lay on the floor. I asked him to let me stay there. He said he'd no authority to do so, and then he left.

When I refused to get up, two soldiers forcibly sat me back

down in the chair and, with one on my left and one on my right, held me in my seat. It was agony. As soon as they stepped away I once more threw myself down. When they came to force me up again, I told them I couldn't stand their torture any more. I pleaded with them to end it by killing me. They must have realised that I genuinely could take no more, and that no matter what they said, I would probably not stay in my seat. They left me lying on the ground.

And so it went on. The nurse continued to administer regular painkillers and they continued to stop me sleeping. Should I so much as shut one eye, they'd come in to beat the ground with their broomsticks while simultaneously shouting at me not to sleep – which was a waste of time since I was shaking so hard with cold that there was no way I could have slept.

I wasn't the only one who was suffering. Although the room was soundproofed, I could hear muffled noises, and when they opened the door, I heard clearly the sound of others being tormented. I heard other prisoners calling to the soldiers and I heard loud, insulting music, Eminem-style, full of swear words. Once I was dragged past one of the interrogation rooms and noticed that the door had the word 'Hell' written on it in Arabic by a soldier, interrogator or interpreter. This told me that not only was I not alone in my ordeal but other prisoners must be having an even worse time than me. This wasn't the only prison I'd been in where someone had written 'Hell' on an interrogation-room door: they'd done it in Bagram as well. I guess it was an expression of soldier humour which, along with their nicknaming the block for mentally disturbed patients the Alfred Hitchcock block, illustrated the pleasure they derived from our misery.

One of my fellow prisoners later described to me how, while he'd been restrained in his chair, soldiers had poured a circle of a chemical liquid around him that gave off an intense and unpleasant smell. He'd had no choice but to breathe in this foul stuff, and when he did white foam came out of his mouth. He passed out, regaining consciousness to find that the soldiers had cleared up the liquid. All this he experienced in addition to my same severe cold, pain and sleep deprivation.

On the fourth day of my torment a uniformed, bespectacled man who must have been watching from behind the smoked glass entered the interrogation room. He demanded to know why I didn't get off the stage and why I'd incited the prisoners and then he left the room. He was followed by a different man, also in uniform (they must have both been from military intelligence since personnel from the CIA, FBI and other agencies came in civilian dress). This one was short and round and also wore glasses, although his had thick lenses that grotesquely magnified his eyes. He tried another tack: he asked why I didn't have mercy on myself by leaving the prisoners to their own devices. 'See what you have brought upon yourself,' he said in a soft voice, which made me understand that, while his colleague was playing the bad cop, this plumper, kinder one had been given the role of a compassionate father who wanted to rescue me from my ordeal. Before he left he told me that as soon as I agreed to stop inciting the other prisoners, they'd stop torturing me. In the meantime they kept me rotating between sessions with the harsh one who threatened me and the sympathetic one who said he wanted to save me.

At the same time, the soldiers stopped me from using the toilet by refusing to respond when I told them I needed to go. Once they held off for so long that I could no longer control myself and soaked my clothes and seat. Despite the humiliation, I told myself that there was some advantage in having done this, because when I got back to my cell with wet clothes, my friends would see what a state I was in and this might make them try and help me.

They hadn't been able to do much so far, but through no fault of their own. They were already suffering badly: they were intimidated and they needed a leader in the block to help them take action. But by making an example of me the interrogators were busy showing my fellows what would happen if anyone else spoke out against them. Nevertheless, I thought that wetting my pants might just provoke a protest.

But it was not to be. As soon as the soldiers saw what had happened they came running in. For the first time they increased the temperature from cold to hot and left me there so my clothes would dry. Only after this, and when I was dry, did they return me to my cell. It was in Camp 2 or 3, but I moved around so much I can't remember which it was.

And so the days passed, with interrogators visiting me daily to check how close I was to surrendering. On the tenth day I decided that I had to find a way out of the agony. When the 'sympathetic' interrogator appeared I told him that I'd learned my lesson and that I'd stop inciting the other prisoners. He was so happy to hear this – his pleasure was clearly visible in his expression as if he had been undergoing torture, not me. This told me what I'd already begun to suspect: that my fortitude in the face of agony, and my insistence on defending our rights, was a great hindrance to them.

The interrogator said I was doing the right thing and that I wouldn't be brought back to this place. That night another officer came to my cell to tell me that the colonel had sent him to congratulate me, to say that they'd never take me to Brown block again and that I'd be allowed to sleep. But first an interrogator wanted to see me in the interrogation room – for discussion purposes only.

In the interrogation room my bad cop was waiting for me. He welcomed me, asking if I wanted coffee. I didn't believe it was a genuine offer but I said yes anyway. And sure enough he did bring coffee as well as nuts and dates which he put on the table before unshackling my hands. Clearly he wanted something from me. So I drank his coffee and ate his nuts and dates and then he told me that he was to be my new interrogator. He began to ask the same kinds of questions I'd answered dozens of times before and then, at last, he sent me back to my cell.

Finally I was allowed to sleep. But the sleep and the warmth I'd so been craving wasn't, as it turned out, going to last long.

13

The Koran protest had been rumbling on all this time and now the camp administration resolved to bring it to an end by returning copies of the Koran to those who'd given them up. We refused to take them back so eventually the officials decided to force them on us. They came with the ERF who began to remove prisoners from their cells one by one. Each Koran was then placed inside the cell before the prisoner was returned to it.

They started this process in a neighbouring block. I sat in my cell listening. I could hear how prisoners were resisting their removal and how the officials, knowing the danger of losing control, were brutal in their response: later I heard that many of the prisoners sustained injuries serious enough to put them in hospital.

I was under heavy guard and didn't move a finger. I didn't want to participate. I couldn't bear being sent back to the torture chamber. But it made no difference what I did or didn't want. They blamed me for what had happened anyway.

Convoys of soldiers moved into our block – at their head the two interrogators who had overseen my torture. They sprayed me with hot gas and ordered me to kneel with my hands on my head. As the gas hit my throat and eyes, my knees buckled and I went down.

The soldiers had already surrounded my cell: now they swooped in. They wanted to demonstrate how great their power was over me and so were particularly vengeful even though I'd done nothing. While prisoners were usually taken from their cells and to the interrogation blocks in a small car, this time more than a dozen soldiers shackled me and dragged me there while simultaneously beating me. They pulled me with such force that the shackles stripped the skin off my ankles, making them bleed profusely. The soldiers were running as they dragged me and the shackles stopped me from being able to keep up so I kept falling on my face. That didn't stop them: they continued to drag me all the way back to Brown block.

I was thrown into the same room where I'd just spent ten hellish days. I couldn't stop myself from shouting: 'Why? What did I do?' But it made no difference what I said. They just went on insisting that I was the instigator of the rebellion. They tortured me worse than ever before. They beat me while my hands and feet were shackled, and when they were returning me to my cell they'd sometimes pull me off the car by the shackles on my feet. I'd fall to the ground and they'd drag me across the gravel.

Every day the bad-cop investigator would ask, 'Why do the prisoners listen to you?' a question he would also repeat before leaving. Sometimes he varied his words by saying, 'Why do the prisoners follow you?' and he would stand there for a few moments, and then disappear until the following day. I knew he was hiding behind the smoked glass, watching me, and I knew it was he who instructed the soldiers to return me to my cell after another eight hours of cold, pain and sleep deprivation. Sometimes the good cop would come in and tell me that I was so smart, I should save myself. Given how transparent they were I began to understand that *they*, on the other hand, were not that smart.

The good cop also asked me why I didn't order the prisoners to take their Korans. I told him that this wasn't in my power, that what went on outside the interrogation room had nothing to do with me. It wasn't true. I knew I could have stopped the protest. But I didn't want to. It had been all my idea and if I stopped it this might indicate to them that I could be bought and they'd end up using me as a spy. This thought terrified me.

The fear was reinforced when the interrogator started to tell me how, having lived in the West, I must be able to understand how 'they' lived and thought, and at the same time, because I was part of and understood Arabic culture, I'd also be able to understand how my brothers, the prisoners, functioned. That meant, he continued, I'd know what they were thinking – something the soldiers couldn't work out. He asked me to act as a bridge between the prisoners and the camp authorities and, to force me into agreement, they took me to another room where the temperature was so low it was like being in a large refrigerator. Then they left me there to freeze.

Even after all this time I can't find words to adequately describe what a terrible state I soon was in. If I could have, I'd have brought an end to my suffering. But what I feared more than their torture was becoming their man. That's what kept me strong.

If, out of my desperation, I agreed to work for them, I'd also be working for them when they let me out of Guantánamo. And say I wanted to change my mind, which I knew is what would happen, where could I hide? They represented the all-powerful America, and if they decided to come after me, their reach would be worldwide. So, if after agreeing to become their man, I changed my mind, I'd be endangering my family. The more I thought of this, the more I thought about my family who I'd left alone, and the more depressed I became. I wanted so much to find a way to stop the pain but I couldn't think how to do it without creating more.

The more sympathetic interrogator came to ask why I wouldn't help them. Despite the fact that, unlike in Kandahar, no interrogator in Guantánamo had ever accused me of having gone to Chechnya, he now told me that if I didn't cooperate, they'd send me to Russia – presumably to answer charges of fighting in a country I'd never actually visited. He added that it would be better if I chose America. Their America.

The things they threw at the prisoners during interrogations had become part of daily conversation in Guantánamo. One prisoner told us they'd actually accused him of being bin Laden's son. Many, including me, were told they'd been trained in al-Qaeda training camps, or had run such camps, or had donated money to run such camps. Most of my fellow prisoners were categorical in their denials. There were some among us who admitted they had been part of al-Qaeda, but there were very few of them, and of course there were some who conceded that they'd fought with the Taliban. But many were like me – accused of things we hadn't done (and the accusations were all so similar it felt like they were just routine) but, locked up as we were, we were in no position to prove our innocence.

By now I knew that the truth had absolutely no impact on our jailers. Their imaginations had already turned me from a cook into a general, and they continued to change their accusations and their myths about me without a single fact to back them up. I was the one whose breakdown had put him in a hospital, but from where I was sitting, shackled by them, it felt like they were the ones impelled by a mad logic that had nothing to do with reality.

The interrogator kept asking me why I mixed with the other prisoners. He tried to flatter me by calling me an intelligent man who should separate myself from them. As he continued, my suspicion that they wanted to use me against the others increased. This made me even more scared, and this was magnified when they began to stop me from doing the one thing that left me with a semblance of calm, which was to pray.

I used to turn towards Mecca and pray while seated in my

shackles and they'd let me do this. But now whenever I turned for prayer they'd rush in and turn me away from Mecca. A female soldier would come also and arrange herself seductively in front of me on the table and light a cigarette, all to stop me praying. If this didn't have the desired effect, other soldiers would come in to shout and beat the ground with their batons until I stopped.

I tried to talk to them. I told them that they'd asked me to stop inciting the prisoners and that I'd accepted this and, by not taking part in the protest about the return of the Korans, I showed that I had stopped. But despite the fact that I'd done nothing, they'd turned me into a hero by dragging me from my cell and beating me in front of the other prisoners. They said they'd done this deliberately so that I could keep my credibility among my friends. This worried me even more: I couldn't betray those who were suffering as much as I was. I resolved that, no matter how severe the cold – my body had already been stiffened by it – or the pain or the sleep deprivation, I'd endure.

On the walls of the interrogation room there were pictures that showed the US military in Afghanistan handing out bags of food to children and women and the elderly. These photos showed the face of a merciful and compassionate army – one of them featured military nurses vaccinating the children of Afghanistan and distributing medicines: they were all of activities that boasted of compassion and humanity. So what, I couldn't help wondering, had happened to these qualities? Had they been plucked from the hearts of these soldiers before they came to the camps of Guantánamo Bay? Or did those cheerful picture smiles simply vanish after the flashes of the cameras had died away?

I tried my best to understand how the consciences of ordinary soldiers let them ill-treat prisoners. My time in Guantánamo helped me realise that a military institution is vulnerable to the abuse of human rights and the torture of human beings because its strict chain of command permits no disobedience. If soldiers don't obey an order, they're punished and demoted, and this is not something an ordinary soldier will risk for the sake of those who, in their eyes, are evil-doers and terrorists, and trained, or so the soldiers believe, to endure pain and suffering. When they looked at us most of them didn't see their fellow human beings: they saw the terrible enemy described to them by their superiors. Their politicians had also convinced them that we had no rights and should never be brought before a court but should spend the rest of our lives in cages. So they dehumanised us, and at the same time convinced themselves that we weren't really suffering. It didn't seem to occur to them that their commanders were making them commit illegal acts that went against any principle of democracy or freedom.

It was nevertheless unimaginable to me how they not only withstood our cries for compassion but also continued to live normal lives. How can a man who is depriving another of sleep retire to his bed and enjoy sleep's bounty? How can he turn in bed to find a more comfortable position, or lean back in his seat to relax when he has spent hours restricting the movement of another human by shackling his hands and feet to a chair and leaving him restricted to one painful position in some cases for up to thirty-six hours? Does such a soldier not end up feeling terribly guilty for what he has done? This is something that, if I were to meet up with those ordinary soldiers again, I'd like to ask them.

My torture and interrogation this time was continuous for twenty-three days. Towards the end they finally mentioned the name al-Qaeda. They said that one of the prisoners had testified that, out of all the other prisoners, I was the only one from al-Qaeda. I was so taken aback I first had to check whether I'd heard correctly. The interrogator confirmed that I had. I asked who this other prisoner was but the interrogator refused to name him. Since the charge was so untrue, it was my guess that the other prisoner didn't exist, but I played along with the interrogator by asking whether I would be correct in my assumption that in order to have identified me this other prisoner must also be a member of al-Qaeda. When the interrogator confirmed this I laughed and said that if, out of the whole of Guantánamo, only the two of us were al-Qaeda members, why didn't they keep us and release all the other innocents? My interrogator reacted very badly to the failure of his own stupid trick. He jumped up, saying, 'You're crazy, you're crazy,' then slammed his way out of the room.

One time, towards the end of this phase of my incarceration, I heard them coming, as they always did, to my cell. It was around 2 a.m. and it was raining heavily. I experienced the usual terror. But this time the soldiers didn't stop in front of my cell. They walked past and went to another prisoner's cell and abused him. My heart calmed. I was so relieved that they'd taken this other man, and not me, out into the torrential rainstorm. And then I began to feel ashamed that I'd derived comfort from somebody else's suffering. Before I could spend too much time berating myself, the clanging sound returned and I knew they'd come for me.

I'd assumed they'd bring a raincoat to protect me from the rain, but I soon realised that my expectations of fairness and humanity would once more be dashed. They were wearing military overcoats but they took me out as I was, and they took me very slowly to the transport vehicle so I got drenched. They knew what they were doing. Slowly they put me on board, and slowly they drove me to the interrogation room.

They wanted me to suffer but, instead, I didn't even try to resist the rain. I let myself sink into the order of the sky, accepting the softness of its soaking with tranquillity. I grew increasingly peaceful as they drove me, still deliberately slowly, under those thunderous skies and I was happy that they didn't notice my serenity. I spent the night in the interrogation room and in the morning they took me back to my cell where sleep overtook me.

A nightmare woke me. I'd dreamed I was back in my old neighbourhood in Tangier and that people had been trying to remove a gas cylinder which had been left in the street and was about to explode. In the dream different people kept picking up the cylinder, but before they could carry it away, they'd drop it and run, scared that it would go off in their hands. When my turn came to pick up the cylinder I was terrified that it would explode. But it didn't and I managed to carry it and throw it away. In the dream I expected a huge explosion but nothing happened: the cylinder, it appeared, had been empty. I woke up, frightened but unscathed, surprised to find that it was afternoon and I was still in my cell. More than two hours must have passed and they hadn't come to take me away.

I mulled over my dream. In that place devoid of good news we prisoners often found solace in dreams. They were the best part of the night and when they were good (we only ever shared these ones) we always hoped they'd come true. Now I decided that my dream had been a signal that my torture sessions had come to an end. I praised Allah.

14

That phase had indeed ended and I was returned to – I think – either Papa or Lima block. But despite my fervent wish that I never again be subjected to so much pain, this was not to be.

There was always something to complain about and I just couldn't stand aside and watch my fellow prisoners suffering without doing something about it. The next incident that sticks in my memory happened after yet another new batch of interrogators rolled out the same old questions and we decided to put a stop to this stupid waste of time by refusing to speak to these new boys. The administration's response was to institute widespread sleep deprivation.

They developed a system of transferring prisoners between cells to keep them awake. When our friend Farooq's turn came, first they strapped him to a chair in the cold interrogation room for thirty-six hours, all the time preventing him from falling asleep. Then they sent him back to his cell, and every time he so much as closed an eye, they'd make him move cell. Then back he would be taken to the interrogation room, there to remain for another thirty-six hours.

We watched our friend enduring this torment until finally we decided we had to do something to try and bring his suffering to an end. So, by way of protest, we withheld our empty paper plates and our plastic spoons, both of which were normally thrown away after use.

When the officials came to find out why we were keeping hold of these items, we told them we wouldn't return them until Farooq was brought back from interrogation and allowed to sleep. They said they'd consider the matter but only after we'd given up the hidden items. When we refused they said they'd use force. We didn't want that, but all twenty-five of us were united in our determination to resist the administration's prioritisation of plates and spoons destined for rubbish over the well-being of our friend Farooq.

The stage was set for confrontation and it soon began. Two divisions of the ERF stomped into our block in their black protective gear. They moved in formation to scare us: all of them raising their feet at the same time and then striking the metal floor with their military boots. This terrifying dance was designed to show us there was no escape.

They arrived when we were collectively engaged in Isha, the evening prayer. They didn't even wait for us to finish: they stormed the cells as we prayed. They were methodical, beginning at cell number 1, then number 2, then 3, and so on. I was in cell number 19, and as I waited for my turn, watching other men being beaten up, I experienced a rising terror. Then at last my turn came. An officer asked me to hand over my plate and spoon. I refused, saying that I stood with the other prisoners. As soon as I'd said this, the soldiers began their fear dance for the nineteenth time.

They opened my cell door. I knew I was going to be beaten and I also knew that if I didn't resist they would go easier on me. But once more something stopped me from taking the easy path. I wanted them to see that they couldn't intimidate me and I wanted them to feel the futility of their viciousness.

Before they'd managed to get fully into my cell, I briefly scuffled with them and somehow managed to push them off me and get outside. I don't know how it happened – there were five of them and only one of me – but it's possible they were tired from their eighteen earlier incursions. I ran into the corridor which was the first time I'd ever occupied that space unshackled or unchained. Although I was scared I was also almost ecstatic that I'd done this, as were my fellow prisoners. I could hear them cheering and beating on the doors of their cells and I knew that they were euphoric at my 'escape'.

The soldiers tried to tackle me to the ground. It was like some insane American football match where one team consisted of five pumped-up men in military kit while the other team was one man in orange. Even the major, who usually avoided direct confrontation, joined in and it was he who, by kicking me in the testicles, managed to bring me down. There I lay in the middle of the corridor as they rained down blows. They hurt me badly but that moment of freedom, and the pleasure it gave my fellow prisoners, made it worthwhile.

It turned into a long night of confrontation. Gas and viciously barking dogs – I'd heard them before but never seen them used – were brought in while ventilation fans and machines that looked like giant vacuum cleaners were turned up loud to drown out our cries. They also shut off our water supply, a precaution they always took when deploying the ERF. Many prisoners were injured, one was badly bitten by the dogs and taken to the Echo segregation block so the rest of us couldn't see his wounds. And all of this because we, as a group, stood by one of our fellows who was being so badly abused.

When they'd finished taking our spoons and plates they looked around for a way to punish us so that we wouldn't do it again. Since we had so little, depriving us of anything was hard. But we did all have ten sheets of toilet paper which we were allowed to keep in our cells. As a collective punishment, the major in charge – the one who had kicked me – ordered his soldiers to take these away.

Before he left for the night the major came to my cell to tell me that they'd made a mistake and they should have killed me. After that I was taken away to Echo block, which was made up of isolation cells.

In Echo there was a large windowless steel room within which was a steel mesh cell similar in size to the usual ones. The prisoner was inside this cell, while in the other half of the space a soldier sat behind a desk and recorded the prisoner's every movement. Both soldier and prisoner were sealed off from the outside, seeing neither natural light nor darkness. It was so unbearable and so boring that the soldiers would rotate every hour.

I was shackled to a chair while they shaved my head and beard. Every time someone went into punishment they shaved his beard and sexually humiliated him, and they did this because they knew that sexuality and the beard were culturally and religiously sensitive areas for Muslims, and they were determined to use this against us.

From then on I'd be making many visits to Echo. Later I was to spend seven months there without a break, but in the beginning I was at least allowed a monthly bit of air when they took me to the communal punishment cells, letting me stay there before returning me to Echo. Echo, which had been built after my arrival in Guantánamo, was only a few minutes' drive from the other camps, but the soldiers tried to fool prisoners into thinking that it was very far away by transferring us in vehicles with blacked-out windows, simultaneously covering our eyes and ears throughout the journey. They'd then drive us about for thirty minutes so we'd think we were being taken somewhere far away.

On one such occasion, the transfer unit that came to ferry me back to Oscar block was different from the usual escort. It comprised a sergeant major and a captain, among the highest-ranking officers responsible for the day-to-day running of

Guantánamo. When the sergeant major came to my cell he told me he was there by order of the colonel, that they were giving me a chance to improve my behaviour, and if I didn't, I'd be held in punishment for a long time. Then they put me in the vehicle with blacked-out windows, but because the sergeant major was new and unaware of procedure, they failed to blindfold me or cover my ears. The sergeant major was inexperienced in other ways. He spoke to me as we were being driven along and expressed surprise at the length of the journey. When he asked his junior why it was taking so long, the man replied that we were almost there.

It was a hot day and even hotter inside the vehicle: I could see the sergeant major's latex gloves leaking perspiration. He asked again how much longer it was going to take and the distressed captain tried a hand signal to tell him that he'd explain later. It was a scene fit for a comedy. I sat trying not to laugh while the driver, separated from us by a screen, had no idea what was going on in the back of his vehicle.

We stopped at the entrance of Camp 4 whose inmates were especially privileged and allowed to wear white rather than orange. The sergeant major told me that if I improved my behaviour by following orders, they'd move me to this place where I'd be given extra food and could play football and mix with other inmates. Thinking that it wasn't worth replying to such stupidity, I held my tongue. The officer then went on to warn me that if I didn't stop 'creating problems' I'd never leave Echo.

I hadn't set out to attract such abuse. It only happened because my knowledge of English put me in the front line and because I couldn't stand watching the ill-treatment of my fellow prisoners right in front of me without protesting and trying to change the situation. That's all it took to become some kind of big-shot terrorist in the eyes of the authorities.

Once a high-ranking official came into the punishment block with a new official he was showing around. The windows to our cells were closed, but I heard them passing by mine and I heard the officer telling the newcomer that 'this is the biggest troublemaker in the camp. He's number 590, the General.' I waited for them to walk back and when I heard them in front of my cell I knocked on the window. When the hatch opened, I asked them whether they thought my mother had borne me only to create problems for them in the camp. The officer slammed the hatch shut and stalked away. I recognised him as the head of the most brutal unit operating in Guantánamo, famous for their hatred of the prisoners.

The nickname I'd been given brought me nothing but trouble. Nothing I said could change their minds. Between us was a huge gulf of misunderstanding because what I saw as an ordinary human response against their mistreatment they saw as major troublemaking. Exaggerating who I was and making me into a fake general let them use me as a scapegoat for everything that happened in the camp. My reputation went before me and there was nothing I could do to change it. Every time a new batch of soldiers arrived, I hoped against hope that this stupid name would have left with the old batch, but no luck: the departing soldiers were always sure to tell their successors about me. The soldiers saw me as a charismatic leadership figure in al-Qaeda just because I commanded respect and authority among my fellow prisoners.

They took it out on me. Once when I was walking while shackled between two soldiers, they tripped me and I fell. I hit my head and it bled profusely, but they gave me no medical attention. Once they slammed the food hatch on the door of my cell onto my middle finger, breaking it. Once they stood in front of my cell and shouted at me. One of them was holding a gas canister the size of a small fire extinguisher behind his back so I couldn't see it. As soon as I neared the door, another soldier who'd crouched down, again so I couldn't see him, lifted up the glass window so that his compatriot could let loose the gas right in my face. This is how they caught me off-guard. It was terrible – I thought I was going to lose my eyesight. I screamed at the top of my voice to try and ease the excruciating pain but this only seemed to give these soldiers more pleasure. At other times they'd bring a petrol generator and place it at my door. The fumes were horrific. I'd have to bury my head inside my shirt and breathe through it.

As a result of all these things, I even tried to change my name in Guantánamo. I noticed that, whenever I was moved to a new block, people immediately knew me as Ahmed the Moroccan who was always resisting and always in trouble, and I felt exposed. So I changed my name to Abu Imran. Normally when a man attaches his name to his son's he will choose the oldest son. But I chose Imran because I was continually worried about his health and conscious also of how I had let him down in his time of need.

I tried always to keep in mind that there was more to me and my life than being held in Guantánamo. I'd try and remind the other prisoners of this as well. I loved to entertain them, particularly in the punishment blocks. They would listen to me as I used words to paint delicious meals for them. I'd ask them to imagine that they were guests at my house in Morocco sitting around a large dining table. I'd begin to describe different types of seafood meals. There'd be fried fish, grilled fish, roasted fish, baked fish; in all, an array of seven different types of fish. I'd help them mentally picture this abundance, all of it arranged on a large round platter and surrounded by smaller dishes filled with different types of salads, potatoes – chipped and wedged – and various sauces to accompany this. I'd sometimes add chicken or lamb to this mental feast, and afterwards I'd describe the huge basket of fruit – peaches and nectarines and oranges and melons and bananas – along with fruit juices and various desserts.

The prisoners loved it. Some of them would pretend they were actually tasting a particular dish and they'd ask me questions about how I'd prepared it. For a moment we'd forget where we were and relax a little. But I was always careful to find an appropriate way to bring them back to the reality of our imprisonment. So, after I'd finished describing our feast, I'd suggest we take a short siesta and would end my show like that, although often after a few hours I'd hear them calling to me: 'Oh Abu Imran, this siesta has been a long one, can we come back to your dining table?' We'd all have a good laugh at this.

In addition to these moments of humour and connection in the standard blocks, I became aware that I was not entirely alone when I was in punishment either. Visitors would come in their dozens, three times a day, after every meal. I'd eagerly await them and, after they pitched up, I'd sit with them and enjoy their company. I could spend long hours with them without becoming bored, for they offered me a hint that normal life still existed. Their presence made me smile and it comforted me. I'd watch them sneaking in so as not to alert the soldiers.

I'm talking about ants. These beautiful creatures would visit me in my metal prison carrying with them hope and life. I'd save food for them. I'd put it in a corner away from the prying eyes of the soldiers: if they saw my visitors they'd either spray them with pesticide or squash them beneath their military boots. If I was caught feeding the ants I knew I'd be punished with either smaller rations or extra days in punishment, but, despite this, I continued to encourage them. I loved to sit and study them and I learned a lot from them. When they came marching in their rows I saw how they helped each other to transport food. All their activity and organisation was achieved with the finest discipline. Watching them would give me a sense of peace and tranquillity. Sometimes I'd save a peanut, splitting the nut in half and putting each half on the floor, flat side down. The ants would come and eat the halves from the inside, leaving the skin. Such was their delicacy that, unless you turned the nut over, you wouldn't have been able to guess it was empty. And they were so intelligent. Whenever I put food in the corner, the first ant to find it would quickly show others the food. Such a valuable lesson: one ant bringing prosperity to its whole nation. I used to think how beautiful the world would be if human beings behaved in this same way.

The second lesson the ants taught me was that, one having found food, all the others would follow its route, without deviating in any way. This, I thought, should also be true of human existence; so if we want to achieve good then we must follow the path of one who has already done so. If you deviate from this proven path you may never achieve the same peace and prosperity. And the ants were so varied in their contributions; some carried small pieces while others carried pieces bigger than themselves. They were such a great example of the benefits of collective action.

These ants were a rare sign of life, and when they appeared animation would creep into the deadness of my solitary cell and, for that moment, I'd feel optimism rather than despair. But their presence also brought danger – when the soldiers inspected my cell, I was always frightened they'd find the ants. I developed a warning system: if I heard a guard on his way, I'd blow on the ants and they'd scatter back to their homes while I got rid of the food. They soon became accustomed to this warning signal, and each time would run from it. Even so, after the soldiers had searched my cell, the first thing I'd look for were the remains of ants. When I didn't find any I'd smile and know that they'd escaped.

15

Guantánamo wasn't a static place. Three years into my stay they opened Camp 4 (a privileged camp) and then Camp 5 and finally, after five years, Camp 6. Camps 5 and 6 were made of concrete and brick, and were supposed to have better facilities – they had, for example, Western flush-type toilets – but because the walls were solid prisoners felt much more isolated. And Camp 5 was its own particular kind of hell, used for prisoners considered to be of high value (although the administration's assessment of what constituted high value kept changing). In this camp, prisoners never got to see any daylight: they were even made to exercise in the dark, and they were given very little food. Those who emerged from 5 told of their suspicions of being drugged. They would, they said, fall asleep for days on end, or find themselves with erections that wouldn't go away: one of them told me he'd found a pill that hadn't dissolved in a drink he'd been given.

And even though nothing changed in the sense that we remained stuck in limbo, the prison administration was continually refining the way they treated us and most of these refinements seemed designed to further punish us. For example, while I was there they opened a new punishment block which they called Romeo and then they hung pictures of Romeo in the rec yards which made it look as if the block was on fire. These, along with other pictures of soldiers expectantly holding batons, were obviously intended to warn prisoners off doing anything that might earn them a stay in Romeo.

The soldiers also used other methods to break us down. Once I was in a punishment block during the month of Ramadan when an escort took away one of the prisoners for interrogation just an hour before Iftar (the moment when that day's fast is over). They shackled him to a chair and then sent in a female soldier who began touching him and sexually assaulting him by rubbing up against him and using pieces of foam to massage him. He was trying so hard to get away from her that he fell and broke one of his teeth. At other times the interrogators would cover the walls of the interrogation room with pornographic images. The prisoner would be brought into the room in the dark and shackled into the chair and then the lights would flare and he would find himself surrounded by these obscene images. Even minors, prisoners who were under sixteen, were subjected to this – one I met had been fifteen. A woman soldier who tried to seduce him told him that if he didn't like women she could always find him some boys. I also heard from a Syrian prisoner how one of the female soldiers did disgusting things with what she said was her menstrual blood.

We Muslims are private about our bodies and they used this against us. Each new arrival to Romeo, for example, would have their shoes and trousers removed. The idea was to target our fierce sense of privacy and honour. Resistance was met with extreme force.

On another occasion when I was in yet another punishment block and we were involved in a protest, they set about removing our clothes. We fought back and so they only managed to strip four or five of us a day, returning the next day to do another batch. Because new prisoners kept joining the block and then, seeing what was happening, also joining in our protest, it took over seven days to remove all our trousers and many prisoners sustained injuries in the process. It was so exhausting; after seven days we no longer had the energy to resist, with the result that newcomers started voluntarily giving up their clothes. Even so, we prisoners found ways round this imposed nakedness. At times of prayer we'd take off our shirts and wear them round our legs while others would pray in their shorts. But there was nothing we could do about the toilet: prisoners on punishment would have to use it naked and without a veil while soldiers, including women soldiers, stared and jeered.

Should a prisoner refuse to remove his own clothes they'd send for an ERF who'd spray him with gas before cutting off his clothes, leaving him either in his shorts or completely naked. I was left naked on a number of occasions, because I always refused to comply with their orders to undress. I'd rather be beaten than be a willing instrument in their humiliation of me. When you resist you might end up bruised and with fewer clothes, but at least you'd have shown that you didn't willingly accept the indignity. But as a result of my decision to resist, I was often subjected to gas attacks and the tearing off of my clothes while I was shackled on the floor. On one occasion I wrestled with one of the soldiers and I managed to lift up his helmet's visor and bite him on his lower jaw until he bled. He was screaming in pain while his fellows beat me, trying to get me to release him. But I kept on fighting for as long as I could. After that they changed the old helmets for new designs that had a clear eye-level plastic window covered by a metallic mesh.

The times when they did manage to deprive me of my clothes were the worst, since I was left naked to fight the extreme cold and the bitter chill of the iron bed. There was no way, apart from using toilet paper, to shield myself. We were given our ten sheets after every meal and I'd save them until I had thirty so I could lie them between my skin and the metal bed. I'd lie very still and on my back the whole night, so I didn't expose the paper, which the soldiers would have confiscated. Since those times I've suffered from sharp pains in my bones, perhaps as a result of the continuous cold I endured.

More disturbing even than the ordinary soldiers' taking away our clothes was a similar punishment meted out by the psych doctors who were supposed to be looking after the mentally ill or those suffering from breakdowns. Using the excuse that they were protecting us by removing any materials which we might use to harm ourselves, they'd order prisoners to be stripped of our clothes, shoes, blankets and sleeping mats. The air conditioning would then be turned up. After five days of this the doctors would return and, keeping up the pretence that what they'd done had been for our good, ask us whether we wanted to harm ourselves or the soldiers. If the answer to these questions was no, the blanket would be returned. The next day, if the answer was still no, the prisoner would be given back his shirt. On the third day, the reward would be trousers, and so this would continue until the prisoner had earned back his shoes.

But should the prisoner, instead of saying no, reply that he'd no need of a doctor because he was not mad, he would be left naked, day after day, until he played the game by admitting to being mentally disturbed and having previously wanted to self-harm: only that would earn him the gradual return of his clothes.

I named those men 'Pinochet's doctors', because General Pinochet had used medical personnel to torture his opponents. These American doctors let themselves be similarly used by the prison administration to justify the treatment meted out: they helped keep up the pretence that what was done to us was somehow connected to our mental imbalance even though this wasn't true.

I spent a considerable amount of my time in Guantánamo being punished for alleged instigation or non-compliance with soldiers' orders or camp rules. But it was almost impossible not to infringe camp rules for there was no set reference point either for soldiers or for prisoners – save, that is, that the prisoners must obey the soldiers at all times. The soldiers were never questioned about their actions and we were always blamed. In not one of the thousands of incidents between prisoner and soldier was a soldier ever charged or punished for any wrong-doing. And for someone like me, who refused to close his eyes to such terrible injustices, solitary was always beckoning. Much of my punishment time I accumulated by taking part in protests. Soon I was only allowed out into the ordinary cells once a month before being sent back to solitary to complete the three-plus years of punishment I'd accrued.

I spent so long sealed up in punishment that visions of the beauty of nature, which had always comforted me, began to fade from memory. In the punishment cells I couldn't take more than three medium-sized steps before finding myself in front of the steel door. I was encased in metal, without a horizon, a sense of life and with nothing to see.

After a while, I invented a technique to give me some respite. In my mind I'd fly out of my cell and into the world that my imagination would summon up for me. I'd fly beyond a make-believe horizon, looking up at the sun, seeing its bright rays. I'd travel elsewhere as well, conjuring up birds and trees, imagining bees collecting nectar from flowers, and this picture would seem so real I'd ache to taste the honey. I'd imagine the colours and scents of different roses so that I wouldn't forget them. I'd fly up into the clouds as they drifted through the sky like ships sailing in the blue stillness and I'd watch as they dispersed. In my mind I could go anywhere. I'd even travel to the moon to bathe in its quiet light. I'd imagine the stars swimming through the darkness of the night. I'd feel their beauty and presence. I'd remember every exquisite sight I'd ever seen: a sunrise, for example, and the way a thin line of faint light would brighten and drive out the darkness of a long night. Then I'd turn my attention to plants pushing aside the soil as they emerged, or fruits as they swelled and grew firm. I didn't neglect leaves either. I loved to remember the way they fell to the ground, so I remembered this on behalf of all those who weren't allowed outside. I'd conjure up the sea as well, and the fish that swam through it, and the corals in their glory. I'd imagine cattle and sheep as they grazed and wonder at the whiteness of their milk even though the grass they ate was green. I'd think about the height of mountains and about everything that contained life.

Every morning and every evening I'd wander in this way until it felt that I was more attached to nature and the universe than before they'd locked me up. Every dawn when I awoke I'd pray for my imagination to push through the guarded doors and the razor wire and take me beyond. It was from this that I drew my strength. When I returned to myself in my cell, I felt like I'd escaped my sorrows for the forty minutes of my imagined trip. The American soldiers had stopped me from going out into the world: well, I could bring the world to me. Nothing could restrict my imagination and nothing could hide the beauty of the universe from my thoughts, and when I thought like this I experienced real joy.

Before my imprisonment I'd paid no great attention to the earth's bounty. But when I was denied everything I began to appreciate its value. I'd never previously valued the darkness of night: I'd simply switch off the light and retire to bed. But when I lost this darkness, when all I had was the annoyance of prison light, that's when I understood the blessing of darkness and its wisdom.

At the same time, I was brought closer to Allah, the creator of these blessings. I'd thank him for giving them to us. These thoughts of nature's bounty had started in Kandahar, and they embedded themselves and developed in my mind until I couldn't do without them. Not a day went by, even when I was under attack, when I didn't ponder the miracle of the world.

Imprisonment, especially imprisonment for no reason and without end, can break a man. But it can also, because there are no distractions, make him think deeply. In Guantánamo I read the Koran as I'd not read it before and so went deeper into my religion. I learned half of the Koran off by heart: other prisoners managed to retain the whole. At the same time I'd also think about my previous life. My cell became a place for me to properly scrutinise my past.

In one three-day period, I remembered everything I'd done from childhood onwards. I looked back at every bad deed I'd ever committed and these filled me with regret. I thought about my mother and my family, and about all the mistakes I'd made. All the things I'd swept under the carpet were now exposed and the thought of them made me weep so hard I couldn't stop. I hid from the soldiers because I didn't want them to see my pain. I was continually monitored so I turned my back and wept silently so the soldiers wouldn't think that they'd broken me. I thought about my son Mohammad and about Imran whom I hadn't been there to help. I felt as if I would never stop crying and I cried for three full days and nights until at last my tears did stop. It was the best thing I could have done. I felt purified, unburdened, reborn, and strengthened by the realisation that weeping, and facing my past, had been the best therapy.

Despite everything the soldiers did to us I still tried to reason with them and on several occasions I actually found myself counselling them. One told me about the manner in which he'd split up from his wife. He told me how he'd climbed into his car and kept driving, away from his wife, intent on starting his new life wherever it was that he ran out of fuel. This particular soldier was a heavy smoker and he told me that he'd tried to give up on many occasions. So I worked out how much he spent each day on smoking, and then I told him how, in a poor country, that money could save an entire family by buying milk for a baby and three meals for the rest. This, I told him, would bring him much more happiness than smoking. I could see by his expression that he was tickled by the propsect, and two days later he told me he'd quit smoking and had contacted a charity to which he was now sending a monthly sum to be spent on a poor family. I was delighted: I'd helped the solider and I'd also helped a family I didn't know – all this from the confines of my cell.

By talking to the soldiers I learned that they weren't all the same: some, not many, were sympathetic to us and I did witness kindnesses. Once, when one of the prisoners was being punished by the removal of his clothes, blanket and mat, I asked a soldier to give the mat back so that even though the prisoner was naked he would have something to lie on. The soldier was worried he'd be punished if he did this but I convinced him to give back the mat until morning. There were also a few soldiers who would give out extra food.

All the soldiers were practising Christians and I'd often find myself talking to them about their faith. I challenged them on their belief that Jesus was the son of God – we Muslims believe in Jesus but only as a human prophet. I likened the idea that Jesus was the son of the deity to believing in Santa Claus. I didn't do this to offend them but rather to explain to them the ways and differences of my religion. And I don't write this now to offend my reader. I write it simply because this line of argument was one of the ways I used to talk to the soldiers.

I wasn't the only one. I was amazed at how many of the prisoners, or at least the ones who spoke English, tried to draw the soldiers to Islam and towards the paradise in which we believe. Despite the mistreatment by our jailers, we still wanted them to share in our eventual rewards: to me this expressed the tolerance of our religion. Not that we convinced many of them. A shackled prisoner is in no position to convince those in power of his ideas or his beliefs.

Some of the soldiers did show interest in Islam, but they kept it secret. There were some who promised me that they'd accept Islam after they left Guantánamo and there were others who uttered the Shahadah prayer that there is no god but Allah and Muhammad is his messenger. It was partly, I think, because they were amazed at how well we withstood adversity. They didn't particularly like their jobs and they showed this by being grim-faced. Whereas we, shackled as we were, were always smiling at each other, and this, and the fact that we were also so steadfast in our worship, seemed to make these soldiers think our faith must be special. After my release a soldier by the name of Terry Holdbrook even wrote, sending his picture and asking if I remembered him because I'd used to talk to him about Islam in 2004 and now he wanted me to know that he'd accepted Islam. And of course I remembered him well: he was memorable because he had hated the way his comrades treated us and, at the same time, he didn't let our orange suits stop him from hearing what we had to say.

Terry Holdbrook's was one of the few soldiers' names I learned. Although every one of them had their name inscribed above their right chest pocket, they placed stickers over the labels to hide them. This the administration told them to do because, or so they said, revealing their names to us would place them in danger. I saw this for what it was – a ploy designed to sow fear in the soldiers' minds so they wouldn't be tempted to get to know us. In addition, nameless soldiers had anonymity in their assaults: if we couldn't identify them, we couldn't complain.

Most of the soldiers believed what they were told: that we were dangerous people; murderers capable of making weapons from nothing. They even removed the paper stickers from the bottles of water we were given. When I asked why, they replied, in all seriousness, that it was because we could make weapons from paper. One of them told me he'd seen this done in one of his training sessions. Soldiers like him were brainwashed – there was no point in trying to talk to them. Military obedience had completely blinded them.

*

Despite my fear of solitary some new infraction or failure to hold my tongue soon led me back to Echo. There I saw that the administration had, once again, changed its methods and now we were watched via a camera fixed to the ceiling of every cell. It had been terrible to have a solider monitoring my every move but this was much worse. Weeks went by without my seeing anybody save the soldier who came three times a day to give me food or medicine, or let me take a walk at night when, again, I wouldn't see a soul other than my unspeaking, unsmiling guard.

I was desperate for distraction. Once I spotted an ant that had fallen into the glass case that housed the camera. This housing was the size and shape of half a basketball and every time the ant tried to climb out it would slip back into the bottom of the smooth glass bowl. I watched it moving frantically in every direction, fighting for its freedom, and I noticed that another ant had already died in the bowl. I wanted to save it but how was I to succeed when soldiers were watching my every movement through this same camera?

The glass cover was attached to the ceiling of the cell. I fashioned a thin string out of toilet tissue and tried to work out how I could get it into the bowl. I spotted another that made its way across the ceiling and into the glass cover, and I saw it come out. This it did three or four times and watching it helped me locate an opening. Luckily this hole was behind the camera lens so I could insert my thin string into the glass and to the bottom. To distract the soldiers, I began to walk up and down my cell. I saw the ant climbing the string but when it was halfway up it went back as if to retrieve the body of its compatriot. Then it climbed the string a second time which this time I pulled out, safely bringing out the ant. I placed it in the corner of my cell alongside its friends who had come for a meal. As for the monitoring soldiers, they failed to spot this rescue operation that had been conducted right in front of their noses.

I took the rescue as a sign that I'd be released and I gave thanks.

But it was not to be. In fact, I ended up spending seven months alone in this cell.

In the beginning they only allowed me a blanket from 11 p.m. to 5 a.m. after which they'd take it away from me so I'd be exposed to bare metal throughout the day. I was surrounded by metal. I saw no daylight save for a thin line of sunlight which would filter in under the door. When I saw this, I knew it was day, and when it faded, I knew it was night. The camp rules stated that a prisoner in solitary should be allowed out one day in every thirty. Not me – they left me in there without a break.

I looked for something, anything, that wasn't man-made to keep hold of. I collected apple pips just so I could look at them. I used to count the seeds in the core, sometimes there were ten or twelve, usually fewer, and I also counted how many chews it took to finish an apple. I could manage five hundred chews in one apple-eating. Once a small piece of gravel that had been stuck to the soldier's boot fell and he didn't notice it. I kept this stone and I'd look at it as proof that life wasn't all metal.

Naturally the longer the solitary confinement continued the more difficult it became. The narrow strip of light glimmering from under the door was no longer enough: life in this prison was just too difficult to tolerate. I felt as if I would burst if they didn't let me out. I began pleading with the soldiers to release me from the coffin, if only for a day, because I couldn't bear it. I asked them to call their sergeant. I wanted to tell him that if they let me out, I'd behave.

They knew I was breaking down but they didn't care. In truth this is what they wanted. I beat the metal doors and walls and shouted to be let out. Instead they sent me to the psych doctors. I told them that if I wasn't let out I'd lose my mind. I knew it was already happening and I wanted to stop the process before it was too late. The doctors gave me an injection – I don't know what it was supposed to do but it stopped me sleeping – before sending me back to Echo. After that, I was so ill I didn't even know what I was saying or doing. They had broken me at last. I had lost my mind.

They took away my clothes and moved me to Delta block where they held me in a cold room reserved for the mentally distressed. At times they'd shackle me, naked and without even shorts, to the iron bed. I lost track of time and what was happening, but I do know that after a while they sent me back to Echo. Despite the fact that I was under the influence of the drugs they had given me, only sleeping with sleeping pills and pumped full of other drugs, they started taking me to interrogation. They were happy to see me in such a terrible state and they spread the news that the General was finished.

I don't remember much of what I did and what I said during the terrible three months of my breakdown. I was out of my mind, apparently saying all manner of wild things which the soldiers then spread around the prison. According to them, and they told me this, as well as telling my lawyer Clive, I had said that not only did I know Osama bin Laden but that I was in fact his superior officer. They wrote this down to pass it on. They didn't write down the other things they also said I had told them, including that a giant snowball was about to envelop the earth and that they should make sure to get their families to leave their homes so as to escape it. They also spread the word that I'd changed my religion and become a Christian. I don't know if this was true, although I do know that I stopped praying for a while and I also know that I would occasionally rip off my own clothes.

It's hard for me to have to bring these memories back and hard also to be told about the things I was said to have done. When I look at that time all I can see is darkness: it was as if I was buried in a grave. I talk about it now because it was part of my experience and because if I'm honest I might be able to help others who suffer from similar illnesses to know that there's nothing to be ashamed of and also that it is possible to recover. And besides, it wasn't unusual for prisoners in Guantánamo to lose their minds. Some regained their mental balance, others didn't.

I was among the lucky ones. My illness shrouded me for three months but then all praise be to Allah it left me and I began to recover my strength and my sense of self. They sent me back to Oscar punishment block in Camp 2 where my friends were so happy to see me back they sang all night in celebration of my recovery and return.

16

In all my time in Guantánamo nobody – no doctor, no guard, no
interrogator – ever said the word 'sorry' to me. And then, three
years into my incarceration, in May 2005, somebody did say it.
It came from the mouth of the lawyer Clive Stafford Smith and it
was almost the first thing he said to me. After introducing himself
he said: 'I'm sorry for what these people have done to you, and I
say this as an American citizen and an American passport-holder,'
although he was originally British.

This magic word shook me. Clive then said that he'd come
to defend me. I'd been told by the soldiers that he'd come to
Guantánamo to offer to act as my lawyer but, like many other
prisoners who had lawyers trying to defend them, I didn't think
he'd be able to do anything for me. I was so convinced they were
never going to let us out that before I met Clive I thought his
presence there was not only a joke but also a ploy designed by
President Bush to manipulate public opinion into thinking that
the rule of law applied in Guantánamo. In fact, I'd only gone to
meet Clive because the other prisoners had told me that lawyers
often brought cakes or biscuits and we might as well have them.

I was honest with him from the start, asking him how he could possibly defend me when, as we were continually told, there was no court in which to present my case. Clive agreed that there was no normal way of conducting a defence but he said that with his help I could use the media to put pressure on the Bush administration by exposing their violations. Then he put food on the table and asked me to please help myself. Please! This was the best word I'd heard after 'sorry'. I ate two tuna sandwiches and drank coffee and then I had some chocolate, and Clive joined me in this feast. Every time I ate one thing, he urged me to eat another. I couldn't stop thanking him.

On the first visit, Clive was around for two or three days, each time bringing food, and as we talked I began to trust him. I told him about my encounters with the interrogators and the American and British intelligence services and how they hadn't even bothered to investigate my case. For the first time someone was actually listening to me.

For Clive's first visits I was shackled with a black belt rather than with the usual chains. But when he came back two months later, I refused the belt and insisted on the chains. The soldiers tried to resist my demand, but when I then refused to meet my lawyer, they gave in and chained me.

The chains had a blue metal attachment which restricted movement and stuck to my hands causing considerable pain. When Clive came in, and I'd been untied, I showed him the blue attachment and the chains and we discovered they'd been made in Britain. I asked him to note the marks these chains made and to see how long they remained visible on my wrists. We sat together for over three hours and the marks were still clearly there. I did this because I wanted Clive to see the ill effects of the shackles and I also wanted him to know that the administration used the black belt to try and hide their normal brutal forms of restraint whenever lawyers or the Red Cross came around.

After that, I told Clive how in July 2001, the time that the Americans alleged I'd been undergoing training at the hands of al-

Qaeda personnel in the camps of Afghanistan – which they claimed they had witnesses to support – I'd actually been a cook in London. I gave him details of the places I'd worked, and the temporary employment agencies I'd used, and he promised to investigate.

Meanwhile the interpreters distributed a document which outlined the latest idea taking shape. The Americans were, the document said, going to form a commission to examine the circumstances and history of every prisoner. Those who were judged not to be enemy combatants would be allowed to leave Guantánamo. The others would continue to be imprisoned until they produced evidence to prove their innocence.

I was summoned to one of the sessions of this commission. They'd dressed a normal interrogation room with a microphone and an American flag, presumably to create the impression of a real courtroom – although unlike in a real court my chosen lawyer was not allowed to be there to represent me. A military officer read out the allegations against me. These claimed that I was an enemy combatant, which was defined as 'an individual who was part of or supporting the Taliban or al-Qaeda forces or associated forces that are engaged in hostilities against the United States or coalition partners. This includes any person who committed a belligerent act or has directly supported hostilities in aid of enemy armed forces.' They accused me of being a member of al-Qaeda and, as apparent evidence detailed, that I'd prayed in two mosques in London which were known for extremism. I'd previously mentioned both these mosques to my interrogator: one was the London Central Mosque and the other was an Islamic welfare centre which had been close to where I'd been living in Finsbury Park. They called these mosques extremist but when I'd first mentioned them they didn't even know where they were. Now they just said whatever they felt like saying.

The charges then detailed what I'd endlessly told them: that I'd gone to Afghanistan then fled in company with a large convoy before being captured. All true but none of it a crime. After that they came up with that old chestnut that I'd been in a training camp in July 2001. They also threw in their previous, and ridiculous, accusation that I'd issued a fatwa making suicide permissible, that I'd been a member of an extremist group of which I'd never heard, and that I'd admitted to knowing how to conduct suicide attacks on airliners using smuggled flammable liquids, which was simply not true.

When the officer finished reading the allegations, I asked him how he could consider me an enemy combatant when the first time I'd seen an American soldier was at the airport in Pakistan while I was in shackles. I said, if they thought I was an enemy combatant, they should at least specify a place where I was supposed to have fought. I also asked how was I supposed to prove I didn't pose a threat to the security of America: instead of being considered innocent until proved guilty as in a normal court of law, in Guantánamo the opposite applied. When I said this, the farce played itself out: in a rage the officer grabbed his papers and slammed his way out of the room, never to return.

My only hope of release was Clive. Later I was to learn how difficult it was for him to prove my innocence. Firstly, anything I told him had to be cleared by the censors before he was allowed to investigate it, and this took three months each time. Then there was the problem that there was no specific allegation against me that he could disprove: initially he was just told that I had been in a camp, but not when. His organisation, Reprieve, therefore set about trying to prove where I'd been for a period of several years which was a very difficult thing to do.

In April 2006, he came back with evidence from the recruitment agency which corroborated what I'd always told my interrogators. Later he proved that I'd been in London in July 2001, which turned out to be the period in question, and this was reinforced by a written statement from another member of staff who'd worked with me. This same man also substantiated what I'd also kept trying to tell them – that due to scarcity of work I'd started looking for a different trade. Clive had found further evidence that I'd transferred money through a post office in London to my bank in Morocco during that July and that I'd made cash withdrawals from my building society in London.

If Clive and Reprieve, many of whose members are volunteers, could uncover all this, why couldn't the all-powerful American and British intelligence agencies do the same thing? Either they hadn't bothered to check my alibi or else they had checked it, found out that it was sound and still continued to detain me.

Not that Clive's proof immediately got me out. I've no idea why it didn't, but I do know that my case was by no means the only one where prisoners were told by their lawyers and even sometimes by their interrogators that they were going to be released, only to have nothing happen.

I had proof of my innocence but they continued to detain me. The evidence didn't help reduce my punishments either. I was their victim and there was nothing I could do about it. Each time they made me offer up my hands for shackling I felt an ever-increasing combination of humiliation and rage that these soldiers, who had no evidence against me, were still detaining me. I kept remembering those scenes of carnage I'd witnessed in Afghanistan, and I also kept remembering that innocent Afghani child who had given me his precious walnuts. Holding up my hands to be cuffed I'd see an image of his hands, and I'd ask myself whether my shackles were a punishment for having taken a handful of walnuts.

The army who'd terrified that child by bombing his country was the same army who were imprisoning someone who had gone there to help feed that child. America wanted the world to know that they were giving assistance to the Afghani people, and yet they couldn't accept that I'd been doing exactly the same thing. We charitable Muslims were not considered human enough to genuinely want to be of help. Instead the Americans had categorised all the Islamic aid organisations and individuals as terrorists who worked under the guise of aiding the poor and the orphaned.

17

Because of our proximity to the sea and the climate, the iron of the cells rusted to such an extent that during my time in Guantánamo everything metal had twice to be rubbed down and renewed. In contrast, our hearts were strong: they didn't rust under the impact of our degradation. We used the smallest thing – paper plates, plastic spoons, even the rust – to resist total domination.

When I was first put in the segregation cells there were slots in the door through which the soldiers could scrutinise the prisoners. These were kept shut unless a soldier wanted to look in, but after a while they were replaced by thick glazed glass that enabled the soldiers to monitor the prisoners at all times. I was by now almost permanently segregated and the prison administration had placed me with four other prisoners, all of whom have since been freed but who then, like me, refused to stay quiet. Once every thirty days we'd be sent to one of the outside blocks for a single day before being taken back. The intention was to keep us separate from the rest of the prison population, including prisoners in the other segregation units, so that we'd have no chance to organise protests. But their plan backfired and ended up lighting a blaze that would have far-reaching consequences and lead to a big change in rules governing the entire prison.

We were ingenious with the little that we had. We communicated by shouting which was exhausting and sometimes got too much, but since this was the only human contact available we persisted. This is how one of us told the rest that he'd picked out a small piece of flaking rust from around his toilet, and, having tried rubbing his windowpane with it, found that the glass was soon so discoloured that the soldiers could no longer see in. We all copied him, rubbing our own panels, encrusting them with rust so completely that they were impossible to clean. When a pane of glass got too bad, they'd move us into a new cell so they could replace it but because these rust flakes were everywhere we'd soon have clouded up the glass in our new cells as well. In response, they got better at replacing the glass, taking us out of our cells for only a short time while they did so. This was the nature of our war: we used the tiniest thing to further protest while they tried to show us that nothing we did could bother them.

But our actions did disturb them. After trying for years to subdue us, they still hadn't succeeded. They had all the power but they were losing their war. This was inevitable since the whole goal of their actions was to convince us that our only choice was total submission which was something many of us were never going to accept.

We became so adaptable in this battle that we used punishment as a way of organising ourselves. After punishment, prisoners were still being sent back not to their old block but to a different one. This system, designed to isolate us, had the opposite effect – punishment became the link between blocks, helping prisoners swap information about what was happening throughout the prison.

Despite this informal information channel it was still hard to coordinate between different blocks and our big dream was to unify the whole prison population in single protest.

In segregation, my four companions and I set ourselves the task of thinking up a campaign that would put pressure on the administration to end the way the psych doctors were complicit in the stripping of the prisoners as well as the humiliation of having to use the toilet without clothes or any other cover and in front of both men and women soldiers. At that time there was constant turmoil in the prison and everyone was exhausted by the never-ending protests and hungers strikes, so it looked like our dream of united action would remain just that. In fact, the current protests were just beginning to die down when the prison administration brought six new prisoners to our block. These six were being punished for destroying their toilets, which they'd done after the soldiers had not only failed to give emergency medical attention to a prisoner, but had also refused to take him to the clinic after he'd started vomiting up blood.

With these new additions we were now eleven. Since they had tried to isolate us original five troublemakers from the rest of the prison I can't understand why they let the new six in. It was a mistake we took full advantage of.

Shouting through the walls, each sharing his opinion, we debated the best way of staging our protest. I'd already been working on an idea for a few weeks – pacing my cell, three steps one way, three steps the other, figuring out my reasoning – so I was prepared. I proposed that we rip up our orange shirts.

Since the main thrust of our protest was to put an end to the punishment of having our clothes forcibly removed, this must have sounded like a peculiar idea. But I laid out my arguments in a methodical manner. I told my fellows that one of the reasons we were prohibited from removing our clothes was because they were visible and helped the soldiers to identify us. If, I argued, we managed to get the bulk of the prison population to join in the removal and destruction of up to five hundred shirts this would not only confuse them but also send a strong signal about our refusal to put up with punishments, and it would undermine the camp authorities who'd given us the orange kit. Since, I continued, it was compulsory for them to clothe us (I told my fellow prisoners that this was written into the Geneva Convention – I didn't know if it was but thought it might be), a prisoner being escorted to interrogation or clinic without a shirt would be an embarrassment to the army. Although we never met them we knew journalists and their like paid frequent visits to the prison and if they were to see us dressed only in our trousers this would make a huge impression. The orange clothes were also a visible sign that we were their prisoners: by removing our shirts we would be sending the administration a message that we were no longer prepared to be their captives. And finally, I argued that if every one of us tore up our shirts at the same time, and if we then tore up any new shirts issued to us, they'd have a serious problem, not least because the Pentagon would start asking why they were spending so much money on shirts.

The other prisoners liked my idea and agreed to it. As was customary at the start of any of our organised protests, we called for a translator and asked him to tell the prison administration that we were going to tear our shirts so as to stop the doctors from ordering that they be removed along with our trousers. Then we did just that – I found the most effective way was to push my fingers into the collar and tear down – and afterwards we gave the pieces to the soldiers to send to the administration. Their response was to tell us that we'd be collectively punished by three days' deprivation of our shirts which amused us and showed just how at a loss the authorities were. On top of this, even before the three days were up, the usual day for washing and changing clothes came around. Despite their grand threats they, as per their usual routine, issued us with fresh shirts. We tore these up as well.

The administration couldn't work out how to deal with this new phenomenon: so again they punished us by depriving us of our shirts, this time for five days! That's when we knew we'd hit upon a way of protesting that was ideal because it drained the administration and not us. Despite the cold, made worse by the lack of shirts, we were euphoric. We decided to continue to tear up our shirts.

To spread word of our protest we had to wait until one of us was allowed to go to the outside blocks for their one day a month. It was my good luck, and the administration's misfortune, that I was first in line. Before they took me out, they offered me a shirt. I accepted it with some enthusiasm: now I could tear it up in front of other prisoners. When I got to the outside block I told the prisoners about our protest and then I tore up my new shirt to show them. There were twenty-one men in this block, and eighteen of them followed suit. And so the shirts campaign spread from the secluded November block to all the other blocks in the camp.

The following day, after I was sent back to November, I was able to tell our group how the other prisoners had joined in. Our actions had rattled the administration. Before the end of the second week of the protest we were visited by Colonel Bumgarner. Bumgarner was commander of the Joint Detention Group, the section responsible for guarding the prisoners and maintaining camp security, and he came to our block alone to try and find a way to end this fast-spreading protest.

He walked past my cell, casually, as if this was a routine visit. I wasn't going to let him get away with that. I began to shout at him, calling him a criminal, a torturer, a violator. He came back and stood near my cell. He looked almost happy, as if I'd been praising rather than insulting him, and this is how I was confirmed in my suspicion that our protest was getting to him and that he'd come to try and find a way out. Still smiling, he asked me why we kept tearing up our shirts, and then he told me that if we had problems I should share them with him and he'd find solutions. He was acting calm.

Once I'd caught my breath, I explained our behaviour, and I also told him that he faced a hopeless situation because we were determined to keep on with the protest. It was their duty, I continued, to provide us with clothes, but it was also our right to protest, and so every time they performed their duty we'd exercise our right and tear up their clothes. Then I described the many ways in which the soldiers infringed our rights, and I talked about the way the rules of the camp offered us absolutely no protection. I added that he let the soldiers violate their own rules by letting them cover up their name tags which meant that we could never file complaints against individuals. When he answered that this concealment was for the soldiers' safety and protection, I asked him about our right to safety and protection. Then I suggested that the soldiers be given numbers instead of names on their uniforms. That way we wouldn't know who they were but, equally, they wouldn't be able operate under the cover of anonymity.

I saw how his eyes flickered at the idea. Instead of letting me finish what I had to say, he suggested that I come, the very next day, with a written list of the demands from our block which we could then discuss in more detail. I told him we weren't allowed pens and so he ordered each one of us be given one. Soon we heroes of the torn shirts, having agreed among ourselves to my negotiating with the colonel, set to writing down our main concerns and our demands. We'd decided that when we were done we'd aggregate the demands so that the authorities wouldn't know which individual had asked for what. And so we set about each making our own list of changes we thought would best serve the interests of the whole prisoner population.

When we'd finished, a soldier collected all the lists and brought them to me. Many of the demands were similar, but some made me cry and some made me laugh. When my friend Rashid from Saudi Arabia, who'd been secluded with me in this block for a number of months, asked for permission to be allowed out more than one day every month, I cried because his request showed that he'd lost hope of ever being released from segregation. The grief I experienced at this request was worse because I felt the same.

Abdullah from Syria was among our original five secluded prisoners, and he had a desperate craving for mixed nuts, so he added this request to his list, a request that made me laugh out loud. After sobbing and laughing, I combined all the main requests into a list of twenty-nine.

At the top of the list were our aims for getting the soldiers to respect our religion. We demanded, for example, that the Koran be respected, that a cone be placed in the middle of each block during times of prayer, that soldiers respect this and refrain from transporting prisoners for a period of twenty minutes around times of prayer, and that they refrain from using our religion to punish us.

We then went on to more general demands that covered the way we were treated. We demanded the abolition of sleep deprivation and extended interrogation sessions, and the abolition of the punishment of removing our clothes and rubber mats at the behest of the psych doctors. We addressed our difficulties concerning interrupted nights by demanding that they stop transporting prisoners between blocks after 10 p.m. and that they dim the lights after 9 p.m. We demanded medical and dental care for all prisoners and, specifically, that Mishal be allowed to move out of the hospital (where he had by now spent over two years) and into Camp 4 (where conditions were more relaxed). We demanded that the soldiers be stopped from calling us 'packages', that they should wear identity numbers on the uniforms which we'd be able to use in lodging complaints after attacks.

We further demanded that those who'd been in the segregation cells for long periods of time (some had spent periods there in excess of two years) be let out into outside blocks so they could see the sun. We also wanted visible wall clocks for every block, longer exercise periods (we were only allowed twenty minutes three times a week), and extra toilet paper (we asked for thirty rather than the usual ten sheets). In addition we demanded that we be allowed to use a curtain or veil when using the toilets or showers, to receive mail from our families (this was kept from prisoners in the punishment blocks), and to get books. We also wanted them to stop the Red Cross from having access to Guantánamo (this was because we'd come to the conclusion that, rather than serving our interests, the Red Cross was providing cover for them to carry on abusing us – we knew this request would never be granted but we thought it would send the message anyway).

We tried our best to make our requests easy to implement. We wanted to win the protest of the shirts and make our lives more bearable.

The following day when they took me to meet with the colonel he had three assistants with him. They included the sergeant major who'd sweated so profusely in the transport vehicle the day I was transported from Echo, as well as a commander and a high-ranking major who was second in command to the colonel. The four of them sat opposite me at a table. About three metres away there was a soldier standing guard.

When they unshackled my hands I put the list down. The colonel then introduced his companions, emphasising that they four were responsible for the field operations of the camp and that they therefore had the authority to amend the rules. This was one of the greatest moments of my life. I'd stood firm and endured all the punishment from the days of Bagram. And now my resolve had borne fruit. After three and a half years they were finally going to listen to us.

I started by saying that if a doctor prescribes medicine for a patient and it doesn't work, common sense dictates the doctor should change the medication. What I was trying to make them understand was that if they wanted the camp to run properly, they'd have to respect our rights and tell their soldiers to keep their hands off us. I wanted them to see that this made sense, so I talked about the way that the succession of generals and colonels who'd tried to run Guantánamo had failed to keep order. This was because they viewed us through the logic of war. But, I said, we were not in a war situation. These earlier commanders, I told them, had lacked the competence to use civilised methods and on top of that they lacked knowledge of the language, culture, customs and religion of the prisoners. It was this ignorance together with their arrogance that made us so angry.

They seemed to understand what I was saying and so we moved on to discuss our list of demands. We spent a while talking about abolishing the forced removal of clothes, the root cause of our current rebellion. I told them that they had no right to take our clothes as punishment and that the psych doctors, who were at Guantánamo to treat patients, should not be party to this.

The colonel asked me to suggest a more suitable punishment and my answer was that their best bet would be to ease the choking rules that created conflict and confrontation instead. I also reiterated my idea of soldiers wearing identity numbers. This would go a long way to helping us believe that should the soldiers abuse us they'd be punished, and it would simultaneously stop us from having to take our defence into our own hands. The colonel again seemed impressed by this idea. To further make my point that a more benign regime would benefit them, I'd prepared a short history of the previous punishments and ripostes that had led to the shirt protest.

We talked for two and a half hours and by the end they'd agreed to our first few requests. They asked me to get my friends to end the shirt protest, but I made it clear this wasn't going to happen until the abolition of the stripping of prisoners was announced. The colonel promised me that he would do this and that we'd continue our discussion the following day.

I got back to find my friends eagerly awaiting me. I told them what had happened and that the colonel had promised he'd end the stripping punishment. At approximately nine o'clock that night the first results of our protest were apparent when they dimmed the lights inside the cells, not only in ours but in all the blocks. And the soldiers gave us each thirty sheets of toilet paper instead of ten as well. That was the best night we'd spent in the segregation cells.

The following day, for the first time in the years of my incarceration, they took me to the dentist. They were trying to make me understand that the colonel was serious about fulfilling our requests. After this I was taken to the colonel and his assistants to continue our discussion. This meeting lasted about three hours and I was speaking for most of it. I highlighted the violations committed by soldiers and officials which had led to such brutality and they listened attentively. We talked about all our issues and also touched on the possibility of improving the food. Over the two days of discussion they agreed to twelve of our demands, the main ones being the abolition of the stripping punishment and a commitment to no longer involve the psych doctors in punishments.

The colonel, who'd only been in charge for two months, said he wanted to turn over a new leaf. He said he'd like the prisoners to choose representatives to interact with the administration and the soldiers, and that there'd be a twice-monthly meeting between these representatives and the administration to discuss any problems that arose. I encouraged him in this proposal, saying it would help create a better atmosphere between soldiers and prisoners. But, I added, I didn't want to be among the representatives.

I was tired. Everything I'd so far endured had taken its toll on me. I wanted a more peaceful life without this constant struggling that led, inevitably, to punishment. I felt I'd done enough and deserved a rest and so I decided to step away. Perhaps this was a mistake on my part but it's what I did.

At the end of the meeting when the colonel suggested we meet the following day to finish discussing our demands, I made the sudden decision that the two meetings, and the gains we'd made, would suffice. I don't know exactly why I decided to stop before we'd gone through our whole list: perhaps it was because I wanted to leave with a winning hand. So I suggested that the colonel should complete the discussions with the new representatives.

When I got back to the block, I was almost flying with the pleasure of having successfully achieved so many of our goals. I told my friends about our gains and also that I'd pulled out of the talks. Some of them argued with my decision, but I stayed firm.

Our protest, and the resulting negotiations, bore fruit throughout the camp. There was to be no more stripping punishment; we were given a full hour's walking time twice a week instead of twenty minutes once a week; the soldiers put numbers on their uniforms to identify themselves; wall clocks were hung in all the blocks; prisoners were not transported after ten o'clock in the evening; the lights were dimmed at sleeping times; prayer cones were placed in every block indicating to the soldiers that they should remain calm for twenty minutes at the time of prayer; and the prisoners were allowed to take the Koran with them when they went for their walks so that it wouldn't be touched in their absence during cell searches. On top of this they curtailed the punishment sentences of those of us in November block and moved us out. The camp administration finally seemed to have got the message that the policy of constant punishment would never work because we, who'd already lost our freedom and been deprived of our children and families, had nothing left to lose.

Despite this victory I was far from satisfied. Yes, it was true that we'd won an unprecedented improvement in our conditions. But what continued to nag at me was the knowledge that, in bargaining with the administration over conditions, we might have inadvertently conveyed the message that if they granted us an improved environment, we'd accept our incarceration without trial. It made me very uneasy. I asked myself what else we could have done, and I told myself that we were undoubtedly in a better position now than before our protest. Even so, I knew that our superficial success would serve to distract us from the main issue of our incarceration: that we were being detained indefinitely in a place that was beyond the reach of the rule of law.

The news of the success of our protest spread through the rest of the prison. Our friends in Camp 5 had gone on hunger strike and the colonel talked to brother Shaker who'd started the strike, asking him to abandon it in exchange for an improvement in conditions at Camp 5 which would be in addition to our twelve agreed gains. Shaker, another intrepid organiser who specialised in hunger strikes and who was called 'the Professor' by the camp administration, realised that prisoner representatives would serve our interests and unify us. He was a man who never tired of trying to alleviate the suffering of the prisoners and to protect them. Now he began to move around his block to convince them to abandon their hunger strike, and in this he was successful. As a gesture of good faith the colonel distributed bottles of water to all the prisoners for the first time and improved the food. He abolished the order of the classes and began to implement what remained of our agreed requests. We were also getting sauces with our meals, as well as chips and hamburgers and cheeseburgers, things we'd not had before.

But there was a catch. This more just way of treating us prisoners wasn't popular with many of the soldiers, officials and interrogators: they thought that the administration had wrongly given in to our demands. With numbers to identify them, the soldiers were no longer inviolable. When they did anything wrong, we could ask to take their numbers, and in order for us to read it, the soldiers had to come close to our wire. They didn't like having to obey our bidding: it took away their feelings of supremacy. Discord began to spread among them, as the interrogators made clear when we were sent to them.

A committee of six prisoner representatives also began further negotiations with the administration, but not for long.

18

My doubts about the wisdom of accepting concessions in exchange for freedom kept mounting and then something happened that made me really furious: the committee of representatives who'd been talking to the colonel came out with an idea of his which was to ask the prisoners whether they wanted to be housed by nation and language, in distinct zones. That infuriated me. It was everything I'd so far fought against. I'd resisted General Miller's order of the classes because I didn't want us to be divided. Now this new idea seemed designed precisely to reinforce such a division. So one day, when I was given the new white styrofoam packages complete with new quality hot food and even cookies, I wrote a note which I put inside the pack before telling the soldier to take the pack quickly to the colonel. Which he did, on the double. My note said: 'You can't buy my freedom with cookies.' And after this I just stopped eating. I was never a good hunger striker because in my first year of Guantánamo I developed a stomach complaint which required me to be on constant medication. As soon as I stopped eating they'd stop my medication and I'd be attacked by sharp pains in my stomach which would grow unbearable. This time I kept up my strike for three days, stopping it because I thought I was going to collapse.

While I was on my solitary hunger strike, the dialogue between the prisoner representatives and the administration began to skew in favour of the soldiers and the interrogators. Colonel Bumgarner was the target of serious criticism by his assistants and by the interrogators who didn't like the idea of giving the prisoners any say at all and who therefore set out to destroy the colonel's initiative. Again this news came to us via our interrogators.

Soon things started to happen that made me deeply suspicious. One of the interrogators summoned our friend Hisham Al Tounsi, better known as 'Hamzah albatal', or the hero, who'd never stopped protesting and who was therefore among those prisoners, like me, who ended up spending most of their time in punishment. As soon as Hamzah had beeen shackled into his chair, the interrogator began to curse and swear and then threw a small fridge, injuring Hamzah. Hamzah had previously been in Camp 5 and now they moved him to Camp 2, which was the biggest camp. In my opinion the move was designed specifically to ignite prisoner anger at the sight of Hamzah's injuries.

Having spent years with my jailers, I'd got to understand their way of thinking and my view is that they were deliberately trying to provoke the prisoners into rioting so they could put a stop to a dialogue they detested. It didn't work: there was anger at the sight of Hamzah's wounds, but there was no organised protest.

So the interrogators tried again. This time they summoned Sa'ad Al Kuwaiti for interrogation. Sa'ad didn't often put himself in trouble's way but after such a long time of being asked the same questions by each new batch of interrogators he, like many of us, was fed up with the game. So when they came for him, he refused to go and so they threatened to take him against his will.

Sa'ad's fellows warned that should force be used, they'd riot. This, I believe, is exactly what the other side wanted. They did force Sa'ad out of his cell and, as predicted, the whole block shook with fury. Everybody was banging on their metal doors, the noise was deafening and it didn't die down for a long time, even after the administration had switched off the lights.

The colonel came to see me. He acted as if he had no idea what could have provoked the uprising. When I told him that by pushing the prisoners they'd got exactly what they'd wanted, he said it hadn't been his doing. I'm pretty sure he was lying. There was a chain in command in the camp which we knew intimately and so we knew it was always the man in charge who authorised the use of force.

This wasn't the first time the administration had broken its promises and now those prisoners who'd been on hunger strike began to think that it had been a mistake to stop. They embarked on a second hunger strike with a more ambitious goal. Instead of protesting the prison's many unfair rules, the hunger strikers, as well as the rest of us, who chose other forms of protest, decided to target the real injury: indefinite incarceration without trial.

We invented a new slogan, 'Release the Hostages', which we wrote on the walls of our cells and everywhere we could including on the plates we returned after meals. This message – that there would be no compromise when it came to our freedom – spread through the camp. We were no longer prepared to be diverted by petty concessions which, we now all realised, was what the prison administration was trying to do.

The colonel declared a state of extreme emergency, and they began to move prisoners to punishment. The colonel had been accused of letting prisoners twist his arm therefore depriving his underlings of their authority. Now he decided to turn the tables and, or at least this is what I think, prove to them that he was still in charge: he stopped talking to the six representatives.

The period of mutual negotiation and calm had lasted a mere twelve days. Now the colonel gave new powers to the soldiers. We were to be subdued with an iron fist.

Instead of acknowledging the positive part we'd played, the

colonel ordered some of the most vocal of us to be sent to Romeo block, an order the soldiers carried out with gusto after first gassing us into submission. In Romeo, they produced large noise machines, like hooters, which they put directly in front of my cell. I was so close I could read the logo on these hooters and also see the manufacturer's name. The noise they made was akin to a roadside drill or giant bulldozer tearing up metal and compressing it. Having covered their own ears with protective earmuffs, the soldiers would switch on these hooters, never failing to send a 'Have a good day' in our direction.

These hooters were kept on for hours. If food arrived, we would have to eat with their blaring. I felt as if my brain was being shaken to bits and my eardrums torn up. Even after the hooting stopped, the sound stayed with me, and I'd continue to feel the pounding along with a pain in my ears for quite a while.

The hooters weren't the only things brought into play. They placed large vacuum cleaners in the front, middle and end of each block along with two hedge trimmers, not to clean the floor or trim the hedges but to deafen and disorientate us. While this was going on the soldiers would hide in their offices at the entrance of each block with their ears protected.

There was also another change that had a drastic effect on us. Since the beginning of my stay in Guantánamo, only officers had been allowed to authorise the use of gas sprays. They'd keep the canisters with them during any assault by the ERF, only bringing them out when they judged it necessary. But after the declaration of the state of emergency, spray cans were issued to ordinary soldiers along with permission to use them when they felt at risk. The result was that the soldiers began to spray us for no reason.

The gas was strong enough to burn your eyes and mouth as well as every contact point on your skin. This feeling of irritation would continue for hours and if you tried to wash the area with water, that would only make it worse. If you got it on your clothes, you would have to remove them.

The soldiers also made us wear mittens and clear polythene face masks to protect them should we try to spit at them. Every time they took us out for a walk or for interrogation they'd make us wear these, and if we refused they'd call the ERF. Previously, such force could only be used with the consent of the colonel or his deputy and a prisoner would be given three warnings first and the chance to discuss his problem with two officials. But after the declaration of the state of emergency, all such rules were abolished. Now any low-ranking soldier had the authority to summon the ERF. So they began to regularly raid the cells and brutalise, and they were free to do so because their officers had stopped visiting or supervising the blocks. Not one was to be seen: all we had were the ordinary soldiers and they were intent on punishing us.

There had always been soldiers who'd breached the stated and accept code of conduct but they used to conceal these infractions. Now they did whatever they wanted, and openly. In fact, they began to enjoy it as if it were entertainment. They'd shout and cheer while they were brutalising us – they sounded like cowboys with their 'yee-has'. There was no escape.

Once, our friend Abu Bakr Al Yemeni was told to weigh himself. Abu Bakr always took part in hunger strikes and as a result he only weighed about forty-seven kilos. Because of the pain in one of his legs, he couldn't stand, but when he told them this they sprayed him with gas while he was lying on his bed. Then six members of an ERF stormed his cell. Before they did so they switched on the hooters and other appliances and created the most enormous noise and they also shut off the water supply to stop us splashing them and closed the windows so that nobody in the other blocks could hear our shouts. Then they began to beat Abu Bakr until he was screaming with pain. They beat his head so many times against the metal sink that his blood spilled everywhere. After this we couldn't hear him screaming any more but only faintly moaning. It seemed like he was unconscious.

There were two cells between my cell and his, but I had a clear view of this assault. Some of the others threw bodily waste at those soldiers but for me this was the first time since I reached Guantánamo that I didn't shout out or beat the walls of my cell. I was paralysed with shock. I looked and I looked. The attack was beyond anything I could do something about. Abu Bakr bled so much they later had to hose down his cell.

He spent over two weeks in hospital, and when he was brought back, his head was stitched and his hand broken and he couldn't stand and all because he'd not been able to obey an instruction to weigh himself. And even after this ferocious attack they didn't leave him alone. They came back after a few days and sprayed him with more gas for no reason whatsoever.

One of the ways I kept myself sane during this terrible time was by telling myself that it was my task to bear testimony to the crimes of the ERF. I watched how, after the state of emergency was declared, they used new methods to get revenge. One of the things they did was paint a black line inside every cell about ninety centimetres from the door. Every time they gave out food or opened the hatch, they'd make the prisoner stand behind the line. They'd only give this instruction once. If the prisoner refused, or didn't move quickly enough, they'd storm his cell and beat him.

This happened to our Tajik friend, Abdel Kahar. It was during the month of Ramadan, a mere few minutes before the call to Maghreb prayer and the breaking of the fast. The soldiers waited until the prayer cone was in the middle of the corridor and then they waited some more. Exactly at the moment of the call to prayer they stormed the block and trampled all over the prayer cone, which according to the new camp rules they were obliged to leave alone for twenty minutes after it was put up. Then they sprayed gas over Abdel Kahar and stormed his cell, beating him, in defiance of our prayer and the breaking of the ritual fast, before they left.

This black line brought increased humiliation. If a prisoner refused or was late in complying when the soldiers came to collect our rubbish, he'd also be subjected to a brutal attack without warning. Even when there was no rubbish to collect, perhaps only a piece of tissue paper or an apple core, the prisoner wouldn't escape the gas if he wasn't behind the line.

They began to distribute a new sort of meal as well, on tissue paper rather than plates, in the punishment blocks. The portions had always been small but now they were even smaller. These meals consisted of two bars, each about the length of a finger and the width of two fingers and weighing about 150 grams. It was a mixture of various foods, mainly beans, cooked dry in an oven and handed out without accompaniment. These bars would cause the intestines to harden, resulting in constipation, especially when the prisoners were on this diet for days. And a curtain around the toilet was forbidden once again. Should a prisoner try to use one of the thin mats as cover, or anything else for that matter, his cell would be stormed and he'd be beaten.

On one occasion they took me for interrogation and put a muzzle over my mouth and nose. In the room, I met an Arab person whom I'd never seen before. He said his name was Zaki and he was the official responsible for cultural affairs, a position that I'd never heard of before. He said his job was to coordinate between the prisoners and the administration to find solutions to their problems.

An officer responsible for cultural affairs, at a time when the prisoners were enduring the most brutal attacks in the history of Guantánamo? A strange position indeed. When he asked them to remove my muzzle, I refused to let them do it. I'd come to the conclusion that this Zaki was helping the Pentagon in its brutality. When he kept asking what difficulties we faced, I demanded to know why he was asking me rather than any of the others. He told me that he'd talked to some of the others, and then mentioned their names and numbers, to which I replied that if he already understood our problems, why hadn't he solved them? I thought all he wanted was for me to tell him about the effects of the increased brutality on us so he could transmit this information to his bosses. I wasn't going to give him that satisfaction.

The escalating violence was their way of trying to force us to withdraw our demands for release and instead concentrate our efforts on calling for better treatment. They also wanted to end the hunger strikes.

A hunger strike is a difficult weapon to control. While it was undoubtedly the most serious form of protest against the administration, it also had serious consequences for us prisoners. Despite its dreariness and the small portions, food was the only quasi-comfort available to us. To go on hunger strike was to deprive yourself of even the taste of food, thus increasing your own suffering. And once the hunger grew and your body began to weaken, you felt as if you'd entered a dark tunnel from which there was no exit. The hunger striker suffered not only the hardships of prison, and the brutality of the soldiers, but also this severe deprivation.

But hunger strikes also meant that the administration was exposed to media scrutiny and they had to continually monitor the strikers and force-feed them.

By this time the latest hunger strike had been going on for three months and still the number of participants was increasing, which was cause for great concern for the prison administration. General Hood, commander of the Joint Task Force and thus in overall command of the whole camp, began to visit the hunger strikers to try and convince them to abandon their protest in return for improvements in camp conditions. What he failed to address, however, was the strikers' main objective – release.

The hospitals began to fill up with strikers who were being force-fed through tubes. Life had become extraordinarily difficult – even more so than before. Since the strike had gone on for so long not all the prisoners were able to keep up, and we who weren't on hunger strike found ourselves in the difficult position of eating beside our fellows who were still refusing food. And the administration improved the quality of our meals. They gave us chips with sauces, including mayonnaise, and yogurt and soft drinks. They even gave us sweets, chocolates and nuts. This did nothing to break the resolve of the strikers: on the contrary, they were pleased to see that their self-sacrifice had benefited their non-hunger-striking compatriots.

Because of my stomach condition I still wasn't striking but as time went on I was increasingly distressed at the way we were being treated. Worse, I began to hear rumours that the lives of the hunger strikers were in danger. I decide to intervene. I requested a meeting with the colonel and I told him that, if he let me into the hospital, I'd try to convince my friends to end their hunger strikes. His reply was that he'd first have to consult his senior officers.

What I didn't know was that the colonel had already embarked on a new strategy to end the hunger strike by force. Two days after our meeting he sent me to Papa which was a non-punishment block. When I got there, it was empty. The colonel told me that the hunger strike was over and that I was in Papa so I could care for the former strikers because they needed help.

Soon the cells around me started to fill with former hunger strikers. The first to arrive was a man from Yemen. I was shocked at the sight of him. His nose was bruised and coated with dried blood and his face was like an empty black sack. He was shaking with fear after what he'd gone through, though he was very pleased to have me looking after him. He was followed by other strikers, all of them looking like men who'd crawled out of their graves. Their eyes were sunken and almost petrified, their bodies stick-thin, and every one of them was similarly bruised around the nose. I knew how strong these prisoners had been before they went on hunger strike, so I could tell that they'd been subjected to something terrible. When I asked what, they told me they'd been moved from the hospital into punishment cells which were extremely cold. There they were strapped into chairs – ones that looked like the chairs used for executions – and soldiers began to violently push thick tubes into their nostrils. These tubes hit their guts before being pulled out by force and then reinserted in the same way. The prisoner would scream in pain but the straps prevented him from moving his head. Once the tubes were reinserted, the soldiers poured approximately six cans of concentrated milk and two bottles of water into a bag connected to the pipes, all of which were pushed very quickly into the stomach. A red laxative liquid used to relieve constipation then followed. After that the prisoner would be left strapped and shackled for two hours. If he vomited the whole operation would be repeated with the addition of straps to keep his mouth closed. Because of the red medicine, prisoners would inevitably soil themselves, but they were not allowed to change or wash their clothes.

This process was repeated twice daily and every time the prisoners cried out in pain they'd be asked why they didn't eat. After the bag had been emptied, the soldiers would pull out the tubes with such force it felt to the prisoners as if their guts were being ripped through their nostrils. Any screams, which were unavoidable, would be met by an injunction to 'eat, eat'. This was how the administration put an end to the hunger strikes.

The following day another group joined us. They told the same harrowing tales. That evening the colonel visited our block. He was visibly pleased with himself: it almost felt as if he wanted me to congratulate him. I asked to speak to him. There were three prisoners still on hunger strike. I warned him that these three were evidently hardened to the soldiers' brutality. I asked that he allow me to persuade them to stop. The colonel was too proud of what he'd achieved: he wouldn't give me the chance. I told him that what he was doing was a crime. I also said that his actions must be supported from on high – I meant senior officials in the Pentagon – and he confirmed this and asked me how I knew.

The three resistant hunger strikers were Ahmed Al Makki, Abdur Rahman Al Madani and Ali Abdullah. Two of them would resist for over three years, regularly being force-fed and becoming icons of resistance. This is what I'd warned the colonel about and so it came to pass: the torch of the hunger strike was still held aloft and shining by those two.

In Papa block I tried my best to help my friends. They were suffering from piles and badly bruised noses, as well as from pains in their throats and abdomens. I asked the clinic for medicine but was given no help. I complained to a senior officer about this negligence but he didn't care. I told him that in my eyes he was 'an uneducated piece of shit', which I did to show him up in front of his juniors. As my reward they took me back to Romeo. After a few days they brought in another prisoner, Mani Al Utaybi, who'd been on hunger strike, and put him in the cell next to mine. I was very happy to have him there.

The first time Mani stepped forward to collect his food he was ordered back behind the black line and so he started refusing food again. I didn't want him to keep on suffering: I asked him to overlook their attempts at humiliations and eat. Out of respect for me, he complied, but then I noticed that although he did take his food, he didn't actually eat it. When I asked him why, he told me that in all the months he'd been on hunger strike they'd tried to entice him by offering all manner of different foods, and now he'd stopped he was being humiliated by being ordered to stand behind a line. At this I realised that I'd made a mistake by asking him to overlook their actions. I begged him to forgive me for having wrongly interfered in his bid to preserve his integrity. I told him that I hadn't meant to and that from that day he would never have to stand behind the line. Then I mobilised the whole block to refuse the indignity of the black line. They agreed and so we went back on hunger strike. I had decided my stomach would have to cope.

On the third day they took me and Mani to Oscar. As usual they shackled me to a chair and shaved my head and beard. Then they put me in cell number 19, opposite the large vacuums and hedge trimmers which stood in the corridor.

Whenever we tried to sing the call to prayer, they'd switch on these appliances and also beat on the doors of our cells with red fire extinguishers. They cursed and swore at us, using the worst words imaginable and telling us that prayer was banned. They did this every time I called out for prayer. I continued undeterred so they filled my cell with gas to make me stop. I was on hunger strike and each time I raised my voice with the prayer call I experienced worse and worse pains in my abdomen. I called out to my friends in the neighbouring cells to take my place in calling out for prayer because I'd neither the energy nor the voice to carry on, but I didn't want to give up. None of them answered. By this silence I knew they must have been gassed as well. So I continued to call out for prayer until I succumbed to the pain and my voice failed.

During our strike there was a female guard who used to knock on my cell door and force me to look at her while she did a slow body-move and took a chocolate out of her pocket. Then, in front of my hungry eyes, she'd unwrap it, slowly open her mouth and put her tongue out suggestively to take the chocolate. It was as if she loved making me watch her eat chocolate while I was in pain. At the time, I couldn't believe my eyes. But if I met her now, I honestly believe I would buy chocolate for her.

They also stopped us from sleeping. They'd knock on our doors every ten minutes and tell us to move and show our skin, an exercise they called skin and movement and which they kept up twenty-four hours a day. They claimed that they were doing this for our safety so that they could be sure we were still alive. There were thirty-six cells in Oscar block and they knocked on the doors of each and every one. If a prisoner didn't respond or didn't move they'd bang on his door with fire extinguishers or release gas into his cell.

Sleep deprivation is the worst kind of torture. Physical torture creates pain but this only lasts for a specified period of time whereas sleep deprivation can be prolonged for days and even weeks on end. True it leaves no marks or injuries or traces in the victim's blood but it harms him psychologically and it also leaves its own scars in the body. It leaves its victim wanting to die.

After days in the intense cold, deprived of sleep and not eating, the pains in my stomach became so severe they took me to the clinic. They wanted to give me an IV and I refused. They sent a trainee nurse who was such an amateur he kept missing the vein. I was shouting to try and get him to stop but I was also incredibly thirsty and they refused to give me any water until I let them put the IV in, which in the end I had to do. After ten days I was in such pain, I stopped my hunger strike.

When I got back to it, the block was like a mass grave. We were all worn out: nobody talked, nobody gave the call to prayer. To those of us eating they'd give us our food on tissue paper and the portions were very small, but it also continued to be so intensely cold that I ended up having to choose between eating this tiny amount or using it to block the vent grille. I could bear the hunger but not the cold, so I wet the food until it was the consistency of dough which I then stuffed into the vent. But should the soldiers discover my blocked unit, which they did, I'd have to bear both the extreme cold and hunger too.

I wasn't the only one who resorted to this tactic: we all took what small measures we could to try and make our life less agonising. A young friend, Yasir, who showed his respect for his elders by calling me Uncle Ahmed, was in the cell opposite mine, cell number 18, and I saw that he'd also blocked his own vent and had been caught at it. The soldiers took him out from his cell at night and came back with a water hose to remove the blockage. They flooded his entire cell and then brought him back, and left him there, one of them saying mockingly, 'Goodnight, Oscar 18.' I watched the whole scene unfold from a small opening near the lights above my bed. Such terrible cruelty: even rocks must be softer than the hearts of those soldiers, for rocks crumble and break while the hearts of these soldiers remained indifferent to our suffering.

After a few days they moved Yasir and Mani to the outside blocks and shifted me into cell 18. This cell was of a new design. Its air-conditioning unit blew cold air with greater force through a twenty-centimetre-wide duct, and this air was so extremely cold I couldn't pass beneath the duct. I spent many weeks in this cell and ended up feeling as if I'd been buried in ice. The desperation to have just one warm night's sleep came to seem more important than freedom.

On top of that, claiming that I'd been praying when they were serving up food, the soldiers deprived me of it. They'd also often storm my cell, leaving me with injuries and nosebleeds. And while I lay restrained and bleeding on the ground, a nurse would come and call out the number of each member of the ERF – those who'd inflicted the injuries on me – to ask them if they were OK. Each in turn would reply: 'Safe, safe,' and then they'd vacate the cell, leaving me bleeding and without giving medical assistance.

The soldiers used to release a liquid chemical into our cells through the overhead air-conditioning units and it was so strong it would melt the paint off whatever it touched. It had a pungent smell which caused headaches, dizziness and vomiting. They used to release this gas and storm the cells for the most trivial of excuses. They'd order a prisoner to look at the ceiling, for example, and should he disobey they'd storm his cell and beat him. Or when there were kit changes they'd give out clothes that were either too big or too small for a particular prisoner. Should he dare to ask for the right size, they'd once more storm the cell and give him a terrible beating.

Among us there was a mentally ill person from Kazakhstan who was always slow to respond to orders. I tried to tell the soldiers that, because of his illness, he couldn't understand what was being asked of him. Once, when the man who called himself the 'officer of cultural affairs' came to the block, he found me attempting to persuade the soldiers not to storm the cell of the mentally ill man, something they had been daily doing. I turned to find the cultural affairs Arab trying to swallow down his laughter: I knew then that this man was helping to pull the strings of the regime of brutality that had been instituted.

The Red Cross couldn't help us. Nobody could. Even so, some of what was happening in Guantánamo did leak out. But I suspect that the things that came to light had been strategically leaked to the media by the Bush administration with the aim of sending a warning to Muslim youth.

To have a place where prisoners could be seen to languish indefinitely without trials or any other rights would put off those who might otherwise have wanted to go to Afghanistan or Iraq. As for the negative impact of this message on America's image: well, this, I'm sure, was seen as something transient which would fade when the media got bored and dropped the story. I am further convinced that the violations in Abu Ghraib were not a scandal that they had wanted to conceal, but part of the same strategy of deterrence. The main focus in the Abu Ghraib scandal was on the sexual abuse – which for Muslims entails an intolerable violation of honour. Another thing convincing me that the scandals were deliberate is that the chain of command in Guantánamo was tight. No soldier could have acted in the way he did without permission or orders from his superiors. He was in fact a human robot, subject always to instruction from his officers. It is therefore inconceivable that the soldiers would have been able to do what they did for long periods of time, and in full view of cameras, without the knowledge and consent of their high-ranking officials.

We were in that limbo not because of what we'd done, but because of a message they wanted to send to all Muslims. This is what my time in Guantánamo taught me.

19

I'd thought things were as bad as they could possibly be but I was wrong. They soon got worse. About three weeks after Yasir, the young man who'd blocked his vent like me, and Mani, my friend who had refused to be humiliated by stepping behind the black line, had been let out of the segregation blocks, the camp was shaken by the news of their deaths, along with the death of another prisoner, Ali Abdullah. Soldiers spread the news to all the blocks, maintaining high security as sadness overcame us.

Those three had been among the finest. They were always ready to help their fellows and they were brave as well. They were men of the highest morals: in the forefront of every protest, they weren't given to despair. In fact, they kept on smiling even in the most difficult circumstances.

The administration claimed that soldiers had found the three hanging in their cells in Alpha block at approximately 1 a.m. In response to these so-called suicides soldiers took away all the extra things we might have in our cells – letters, photographs and the like – and they continued doing this for months. They didn't seem sad: the opposite in fact. I kept seeing happiness in some of their expressions, particularly in the faces of those soldiers who were known for their brutality against those prisoners in punishment. It was almost as if they were enjoying the three deaths.

We prisoners refused to accept that the three had killed themselves. We couldn't understand how it could possibly have happened given that four soldiers were supposed to always be patrolling the blocks and monitoring us. Mani had also been on a list, that the interrogators had shown him, to be released.

We believed their deaths were a direct result of torture and were enraged when the administration said they'd committed suicide as part of their war against the USA, which once again made America look like the victim and us look like the aggressors. Rear Admiral Harry Harris actually went as far as to call the deaths 'an asymmetric act of war'. Such cruelty tells you much about the people in charge of Guantánamo for, even if the men had killed themselves, Colonel Bumgarner had been in charge of their well-being and should therefore have been held responsible for their deaths.

These were not the only deaths in Guantánamo. Later the prison administration announced the suicide of Abdul Rahman, another Saudi national, one of the veteran hunger strikers in Camp 5. They gave no details except to say that he was found not breathing. My experience of Camp 5 told me that it would be impossible for anyone to hang themselves there. The cells there had been designed to prevent suicide or self-harm – the walls were made of concrete and there was no hoop, ring or opening to which a prisoner could tie anything.

And then, later still, the prison administration announced the suicide of another prisoner, Mohammad Abdullah Saleh, a Yemeni. Again, no further details were supplied other than to say he was found not breathing.

The families of these prisoners deserve justice. President Bush and his cabinet should be made to bear the responsibility for these deaths of prisoners who were being held illegally without trial.

*

After the deaths of the three brothers, God bless them, I was moved to Camp 5 with its cells of concrete that were entirely sealed in. In the middle of the rear wall was a long thin window of opaque glass which let in some light while still restricting vision. I spent approximately seven months in this place and I found an area about the size of a matchstick in the top corner of this window which wasn't clouded. I'd stand on my concrete bed and look through this hole, beyond the walls and the concertina wire, to the rays of the sun, the blue sky, the clouds and even the birds, trees and hills. I counted myself lucky to be able to see something of the outside world through this eyelet of a needle. After all those years in segregation imagining a natural morning and evening so I wouldn't forget them, I was happy to see these things for real. I'd have to stop myself from looking for too long. I'd climb down from my bed, fearful that I might somehow alert the soldiers who would then close this tiny window onto the real world.

There was another window in the door but its pane was clear so the soldiers could always see in. Sometimes delegations would arrive in the block and we'd always know they were on their way when the soldiers covered the panes with coloured plastic so that we couldn't see out and the visitors couldn't see in.

There was nothing to do in Camp 5 and they'd only take prisoners for exercise at night once a week for twenty minutes. And this exercise would be held in a space a mere 22 feet long and 11 feet wide.

I was in Camp 5 for seven months and then, when Camp 6 was opened, I was among the first prisoners to go there. This is how life was in Guantánamo, from prison to prison, from camp to camp.

Even so, the best things can happen in the worst of places. When I was in Camp 6 I received 280 letters in one month and I'm sure that, because they used to conceal the existence of letters from us, I must have been sent many more. The letters I did receive came from the UK, America and Canada, among other countries. They came from people who sympathised with my plight not because they were Arabs, or Muslims, but because they were against everything that Guantánamo stood for. Some of these letters were from university students in the UK, or schoolchildren, or ordinary women and men. There was even one from a mayor of a UK city and his wife. Another was from two children aged seven and nine: I considered it a great honour that their parents saw in us prisoners of Guantánamo an example for their children. All these letters, which told me I wasn't alone, had an amazing effect on my morale.

I couldn't tell them then but I can tell them now how thankful I was and always will be to those who stood up for us in Guantánamo and so stood up for the principle of justice. Thank you all. Your letters told me that there were people who had the courage to defy George Bush's famous intimidation that 'You are either with us or with the terrorists', and to know that by standing up for us, you were actually standing up for human rights.

The walls of Camp 6 were concrete but the cells inside were metal. There were two levels, the lower ones having concrete floors while the cells on the upper level were all metal. There were three or four showers in the middle of the block. Here, in this new-build block, we encountered the same difficulties that we'd faced for years, especially during the days of the state of emergency. Covering yourself in the showers or the toilets inside the cells was prohibited. At one time they'd allowed a curtain up to half of the height of the cell wall to be used in the toilet or shower, but since camp rules now incorporated the right of the soliders to change them whenever they saw fit, the rules were of no use to us. Even the right to take the Koran with us while walking, which we had won through the shirt protest as part of our twenty-nine requests, didn't apply in Camp 6.

To the outside eye, Camp 6 might have looked like a decent enough place but its up-to-date facilities were only for show. The prisoners weren't permitted to sit around the steel tables that stood in the middle of the block to suggest to visiting journalists that we socialised there. Only soldiers were allowed to use them, and they'd often gather around them while we ate our meals alone in our cells. And although there was a large patch of ground that seemed to be there for exercise, we were never allowed on it. Instead we had to walk down long, thin cages for our exercise hour. These cages were made of wire but eight-metre-high concrete stood beside the wire walls and darkened them. Camp rules forbade prisoners from touching the wire, a rule that was designed to prevent the prisoners from getting any exercise because if you accidentally touched it you'd immediately be sent back to your cell. Refusal to comply with an order to leave would result in a your being gassed and attacked by the ERF.

When they took a prisoner to the clinic or for interrogation inside the prison, they'd put on blindfolds, earmuffs and face muzzles before dragging the unlucky prisoner through the corridors. They did this not because we posed a security risk against which they must take precautions but because they knew that to be shackled, blindfolded and muffled in this manner was terrifying.

The prison administration had learned from its past mistakes. It no longer operated a specific block for punishments through which prisoners from other blocks would be moved thus serving as our channel of communication. Now we were made to undergo punishment inside our same block which stopped the flow of information between blocks.

Our energy had been so depleted by our protests and strikes, I guess they thought they'd beaten us. But they hadn't and soon their escalating brutality recharged our determination. Even those who in the past had never confronted the soldiers now erupted.

Past experience had taught us that it was the administration who chose the type of conflict and who created the right conditions for it to occur. Instead of this we decided to choose and plan our own conflicts. Our main objective was still our release. This we now tried to push forward not by hunger strikes, which had caused us so much difficulty, but by a campaign of disobedience against the rules. We chose this because having seen how delegations, including the media, visited Camp 6, we knew adverse publicity was the administration's Achilles heel and so we decided to embarrass them.

First step: we were going to refuse to give up our hands for shackling. Second: we would refuse to leave our cells either for walking or for inspection. Third: we would no longer return our plates and spoons after meals. This last we decided on because we knew that the ERF would be called on to storm our cells every time we disobeyed orders. So if we held back our spoons and plates it would mean they'd have to storm twenty cells three times a day, and then storm twenty cells again for the refusal of inspection or to go walking, and this continuous action was something they couldn't possibly sustain. Which was our whole idea: we were going to create total chaos.

The prison administration, who constantly eavesdropped on us, knew of our plan. We didn't anyway try to hide it from them. We wanted them to know what we were planning because that way they'd know that they couldn't avoid the confrontation or defeat us in it. The more we talked about it, the clearer it became. We would intentionally provoke the ERF. The administration tried to avoid such confrontations because they knew that the more frequently the ERF hit us, the less scared of them we became. Despite their numbers and their protective gear, if we found the courage to fight back they'd also get injured, some bloodily so. I was among those who took them on. I'd ignore the group and concentrate on one man and soon the other soldiers would have to start beating me off their friend. For this reason, they tended to avoid coming into my cell. If all prisoners then acted in a similar way, the ERF would lose their authority.

And so began a concerted fightback. On one occasion they stormed the exercise cage and beat and removed a prisoner after he'd touched the wire. I was so furious I decided to take action. I'd already hidden a plastic bottle of water in my cell behind the door. Now I brought it out and showed it to them. When they asked for it back, I told them that if they wanted it they'd have to do the same thing they'd just done to my friend in the exercise cage. So they called the ERF and for the first time since I'd arrived in Camp 6 my cell was stormed. And this storming didn't go their way. When they released the gas it was my good fortune that the spray nozzle didn't work so that what came out was a liquid, which didn't have the same effect as the gas would have done. I pretended I was choking and fell to the ground. I heard them say, 'He's down, he's down,' and I readied myself. When they opened the door I sprang up, aiming my blows at their faces. I managed to break off the metal mesh covering the visor of the helmet of one of the soldiers and also to tear the shin protector off another. In the end they beat me down, and they beat me mercilessly, before they left my cell. Still, when they did one of them was carrying his helmet and another his shin protector, and the whole scene had thoroughly entertained my fellow prisoners. In this way, we showed them what might happen if they used force against us and they began to be more reluctant about bringing out the ERF.

Some other prisoners had also started to stage their own individual rebellions. Fawzi Al Kuwaiti, who loved to walk, initiated one. He had a thin physique as a result of taking part in the hunger strikes. Even so, he tended not to confront soldiers head on, choosing to avoid them instead. But in Camp 6 after the soldiers had annoyed him in the exercise cage and tried to remove him by force he resisted and scrapped with them. From this day onwards, after he'd tasted both the sweetness and the pain of rebellion, he set himself on a path of disobedience.

These incidents happened because individuals just reacted. At the same time we kept on discussing our intention to start another campaign of mass disobedience. When Fawzi disobeyed them again during his exercise period, I joined in from my cell, as did Ahmed Omar from Yemen. Ahmed Omar covered the window of his door with tissue paper so as to attract the ERF – they were always sent for if the soldiers couldn't see in. They came in a hurry, and, having beaten Fawzi, they then stormed Ahmed Omar's cell. Before they could finish with him, I had also covered my window with tissue paper. I was trying to lure them in. But they turned a blind eye. They must have been worried that the whole block would join in our disobedience if they also attacked me. I took down the tissue paper and got hold of another bottle of water, which I'd hidden behind the door thinking they would surely have to storm my cell to get it back especially since, as one of my punishments, I was forbidden to keep water.

They switched the lights off and the noise machines on and they also turned off the water so we couldn't splash them and couldn't wash any gas away. Since they always did this before they stormed the cells, I prepared myself, tying a towel around my head in expectation of the onrush of gas. I began to stride around my cell, readying myself for the attack. I started doing this at 9 p.m. and they left me to it, watching me walk around like this until 1 a.m. I was tired. I lay down on the bed. As soon as I did an official came with an interpreter who asked me to return the bottle and in exchange they'd turn the water supply back on to the entire block and also reduce the bright lighting and turn off the annoying sounds. When I realised that I'd accomplished four hours of defiance without the intervention of the ERF, I knew that this would show the administration they wouldn't be able to resist a mass rebellion. So I gave them back my water bottle and in response they did switch on the water supply, turn off the noise-making machines and dim the lights. Calm returned to the cells and we were able to get some sleep.

At 8 a.m. the following day I was escorted to interrogation. I assumed they were going to speak with me about my disobedience. But when I got there I found a group of civilians and military personnel with cameras waiting for me.

Instead of the usual hard furniture there was a desk and two sofas in this room and I was asked to sit on one of the sofas. And instead of starting in the usual manner with questions I'd answered hundreds of times before, one of the men quickly came out with: 'You're going to leave Guantánamo.'

I was totally unprepared, especially after my night of rebellion and waiting for the ERF. I bit back the joy that had begun to flood though me and let scepticism take its place. It was a trick, I thought, another way of raising my hopes only to destroy them. I'd heard of prisoners who'd been told that they were going to be released, who'd even been given new clothes and taken to the airport, only to be informed that the intelligence service had found evidence to show that they'd been lying, and so they were taken back for a fresh round of interrogation and investigation. This trick had resulted in some of these prisoners losing their minds. I told myself I wasn't going to fall into this same trap.

A doctor gave me a quick physical, part of which was to ask me whether I was suffering from any illness that might prevent me from leaving Guantánamo. The question made me laugh out loud. Then they took my fingerprints and scanned my irises and my voice before asking me for my size in clothes and shoes. I kept wondering whether this was a ploy or whether it could be true that they'd finally had enough and wanted rid of me. As the hours passed I began to believe I really was going home.

Despite my years of incarceration, I'd never given up looking forward to the day when I would go back to my family. Every time they took me to the barber I wanted to resist his butchery because in case of release I didn't want to leave prison looking deformed. Now my fears were proven true: I was subjected to the punishment of a deliberately uneven cut to both beard and hair. But despite this I was very happy, particularly since my release had come after I'd stood up so strongly against them.

The news of a release would normally be greeted by celebrations, including singing and poetry recitation, which would go on every night until the prisoner finally left the block. But when I was told I was going to leave, we were in the middle of our campaign of disobedience and the block could barely catch its breath between constant assaults and confrontations. It was as if destiny had decreed that my farewell was to be celebrated with rebellion rather than with songs and poems.

I was taken to a huge outside enclosure the size of a football field where two men from the Red Cross were waiting for me. One of them, whom I'd met previously, told me I'd been cleared for release. He then explained that they were there in case I didn't want to go home for fear of being tortured: if this were so, they'd stop my transfer. I asked them how they could possibly talk to me about torture when I'd spent more than five years being degraded and dehumanised. I went on to say that in all my time there, they'd done nothing to stop what was being done to me, but now that my ordeal was almost over and I was looking forward to seeing my loved ones, they had the temerity to warn me that I should be afraid. I asked them who they thought they were talking to and then I wondered out loud whether they weren't trying to wipe out the violations of my jailers.

The second Red Cross man started to apologise and he did so repeatedly. He was sorry, he said, that his colleague hadn't expressed their concern sufficiently. I replied that I, like many other prisoners, thought that visits from the Red Cross gave legitimacy to Guantánamo and helped conceal the violations that were taking place daily. After all, once when I was in Oscar block and the Red Cross paid one of their visits, we told them how we were being treated – about the sleep deprivation, the cold, the chemicals and how they stopped us praying. The appliances used to create noise were there in the middle of the block in clear view of the Red Cross representatives but still nothing changed after their visit. So I told these two Red Cross representatives that if they really cared about what was happening in the prison, the only way they could help was to refuse to visit.

A week passed and then the day of my release finally dawned.

It was painful to bid farewell to my friends. We had lived together for five years and four months, enduring much cruelty. This is what we had in common and it bound us together more closely than any family. We were like one body. I saw my fellow prisoners crying to see me go and I too wanted to cry. But I held back my tears. I apologised to them, saying that, even at the moment of my release, I didn't want the soldiers to see me crying because they might think that my tears were a result of my escape from them. They weren't: they were for my friends left behind.

The soldiers shackled me and put earmuffs on me and then a blindfold, face muzzle and face mask. These moments were filled with a strange mixture of emotions: the sorrow of separation, the joy of release and the sense of victory through steadfastness. It was difficult for me to contain all these feelings at one moment. As for my friends, as I went, I could hear them singing, 'Farewell to you, oh champion . . .'

As they took me out of the block, I was fighting back tears. When the soldiers pulled me along the corridor, the face muzzle grew increasingly uncomfortable. I tried to lower my head to my hands, which were shackled to my waist, so as to adjust the muzzle. I'd known that my release would be hard on those soldiers who wouldn't have wanted me to leave Guantánamo safely. Now they showed their rage by grabbing me aggressively and slamming me hard into the wall. They tightened my shackles and smashed my head against the wall again. Despite the pain, I didn't shout out. I told myself to bear this, their final opportunity to assault me. I don't know how many there were but I could feel them crowding round, pushing against each other so that each one of them could land his last punch. This is how the soldiers of Guantánamo, like the soldiers of Kandahar, bid me farewell: with beatings. My friends, soon to be left behind, would have heard what was happening to me in the corridor.

Next they put me in a segregation cell. It was evening. They brought me white shoes and white clothes – these were worn by prisoners who, being compliant, were allowed to live in Camp 4. It was the first time I'd worn these white clothes and destiny had decreed that I'd wear them without the consent of the interrogators and inside the segregation block where I'd served about four years of punishment. This was a lesson and an honour for me. I felt very proud of the way I'd stood up for all our rights.

I ate the last meal – a vegetarian concoction of yellow courgettes, tomatoes and chickpeas. When I had finished they took me to a white bus and then they took off my face mask, earmuffs, muzzle and blindfold. I saw a translator and an Afghani prisoner who, also in white clothes, was being released with me, while the rest of the bus was packed with soldiers. One of them stared at me without stopping for the entire duration of the journey. It was as though he wanted to kill me with his eyes.

At the airport I was put on board a military cargo aircraft. Once more I was made to wear earmuffs, blindfold, muzzle, and once more I was searched. This search was humiliating, done, I am sure, out of revenge and the regret that this would be their last chance to do this to me. This time I didn't hold my tongue. I swore at them, using the longest, most offensive words I could, and they deserved every one of them. They shackled me to a long aircraft bench.

And then came the fear that had haunted me throughout my captivity. Every time I had thought about my release and my return to my family I'd remember the torturous journey I'd undergone from Kandahar to Guantánamo. It had been engraved in my mind as the worst day of my life. I was afraid the same thing would happen when I left Guantánamo.

Our journey began around 11 p.m. The only prisoners were me and the Afghani. I asked the flight officer to tell me when it was dawn so that I could pray the Fajr prayer. Every time I asked to speak to this flight officer, two soldiers would come to stand on either side of me and press with their hands on my shoulders and knees before the flight official, who stood at some distance from me, spoke. I couldn't bear these hands on me – so unnecessary what with the chains, shackles, rope belts, blindfold, earmuffs and muzzle. I was very uncomfortable.

Given that I was on my way home, I could have held my tongue. But I decided that I wouldn't, especially in the face of security measures that were completely unnecessay. I'd learned how to defend myself in Guantánamo. The next time they pressed me, I surprised them by taking off my blindfold. I shouted at the senior officer: 'Why are these soldiers putting their hands and their heavy bodies against me? Are these chains and shackles not enough?' I expected them to beat me for having removed my blindfold. To my surprise the senior officer spoke calmly, asking me respectfully to put it back on. When I said that I'd wear it on condition that the soldiers kept their hands off me, he agreed. So I put the blindfold on and rid myself of the hands of these soldiers.

The journey took about eight hours and it wasn't as bad as I'd feared. This was it. I was free.

20

I'd lived for the day when I would return to Morocco and my family. At times I'd close my eyes and imagine I was in Tangier, only half an hour's walk from my house. I'd begin by walking towards my house, passing by the beach. I'd enter the small streets of the suburb where I lived, heart beating as I ached to see my mother, my children, my wife and the rest of my family. Neighbours would spot me and greet me – to them, I imagined, I'd be a returning hero. But I would push on, intent on seeing my loved ones.

I'd ask myself who'd be the first I'd spot. Would it be Mohammad, much taller and more grown up, playing in the street near the front door? Or would it be Imran whom I'd last seen when he was about two years old and whom I'd aged in my mind but still wasn't sure that I'd know? I knew their mother, my beloved wife, would be inside the house, waiting as she'd waited throughout the long years. But before I went in to see her, would my sons recognise me or would I have to introduce myself as their father? And if they didn't know where I'd been, and I didn't think they would, how would I explain why I hadn't come to visit them, and why I'd now pitched up without any gifts for them?

But before I got to hug and hold my family, I'd dreamed about seeing my country again. I'd so looked forward to my first glimpse of its sun, its skies and its sea. I'd try and imagine which season it would be. I hoped that it would be in my favourite season, spring, and I was in fact released on 24 April.

When I arrived at Casablanca airport, in the same military plane, I was met by the security services. I felt someone take my hand as I neared the door of the aircraft and whisper to me: 'All praise be to Allah for your safety and welcome to your country.'

I was put in a vehicle with some people I couldn't see because my eyes were now covered by smoked goggles. I told my guards that I'd been so eagerly awaiting the moment when I'd see the sky, the sun, the trees of my country again, but because of the goggles all of this was completely obscured. At this, one of my guards removed the goggles and I saw that there were three of them. I thanked them for their mercy. I stared out of the window. I felt that I'd been shackled in a coffin for the last five and a half years and now my sight had been given back to me.

The first thing I saw was a cart full of watermelons. Before, in London, watermelons had been instrumental in giving me the confidence to start cooking again, and now the sight of them made me feel as if I'd been born again. The road was also crowded with traffic and pedestrians. I heard the noise of engines, of horns, the general clatter of the roads which is generally considered a nuisance. To me it sounded like music. It made my heart beat fast and all I asked was to hear more. I apologised to the security people for being so preoccupied by these sounds instead of speaking to them but I explained I'd been waiting to catch a glimpse of the outside world for a very long time. They laughed and told me to go ahead and look and listen for as long as I wanted.

They took me to an interrogation centre where one of my interrogators promised me that I'd go back to my home in a few days. Throughout my stay this same man kept promising me that I'd soon see my son Imran. After a week I was taken to the court

in the town of Sela. As I waited in a big hall I spotted a lady
holding her small child in her lap. This was the first infant I'd
seen in over five and a half years. My eyes fixed into a stare as if
I'd never seen a child, so much so that the mother noticed and I
began to worry that I might be scaring her.

Only a few days previously I'd been in my metal cell in
Guantánamo hiding apple seeds and small stones so I could
remind myself of the existence of life elsewhere. Now I was
looking at a child in the safety of his mother's lap. I was full of
hope for a new life and this increased when I also saw a cat – what
a marvellous creature – crossing the hall.

I was taken into a room where a judge sat behind a desk with
his secretary beside him. This hearing was just part of protocol
expected of the Moroccans, and the judge had clearly already
decided what he was going to do with me. For a brief fifteen
minutes he asked me questions with his secretary noting down
my answers. Then he told me that he was going to release me.

I was free. In a state of utter excitement I took my first steps
without shackles or chains. Carrying my prison bag, I stopped at a
public telephone. I tried to remember my number. I remembered
three or four digits but they weren't in the right sequence. I
pressed my fingers against the keypad trying to recall the order,
but each time I'd hear an automated voice telling me that the
number I had dialled had not been recognised. Still, I felt close
to my family because at least I was dialling a Tangier number
where they lived. But I was also worried about how I was going
to break the news of my release to my mother. I worried that the
shock, even if it was a shock of happiness, would affect her health.
I resolved that I'd not say anything about my pain and suffering
over the years.

At last I managed to dial the right number and I heard a
voice: 'Hello, yes?' It was my mother. I said: 'It's Ahmed,' only
to hear her reply: 'Mr Ahmed who?' I told her that I was her
son Ahmed, repeating it, 'your son, Ahmed'. I heard her quiet

voice: 'My beloved Ahmed, my beloved Ahmed.' I told her not to get excited because I didn't want anything bad to happen to her . She said, 'Alhamdulillah [All praise be for Allah], where are you?' I told her I was in Morocco and that I was fine. Then my wife took the phone from my mother, uttering similar words, and after that my sister took over and she burst into tears. Then my son Mohammad came on to say: 'Where are you, Father? where are you?' and he was followed by Imran who began to cry as he kept repeating: 'Where are you, Daddy, come quickly, I want to see you, I want to see what you look like, when are you coming, I haven't seen you, Daddy.' This was the moment, when he said, 'I haven't seen you, Daddy,' that I broke down. I couldn't help myself.

My brother came to pick me up. Contrary to my previous fantasies, I didn't want to progress proudly and slowly through my old haunts and in full sight of everybody. I just wanted to go home as quickly and quietly as I could. We reached my house at about ten o'clock in the evening. I was hugging everybody and everybody was hugging me back as I tried my best not to cry in front of them. I didn't want them to know about the brutality I'd suffered over such an extended time. I didn't want to make them sad by crying myself, but they cried anyway. I took my son Imran, who didn't remember me at all, in my arms. I asked about his medical condition which had worried me throughout the years of my imprisonment. For me this was the moment when the truth of my faith, and my expectations of Allah, were fulfilled. I'd left Imran in his care. All the time I was in Guantánamo I'd told myself that if I held firm, and held my faith, and survived, Allah would repay me. And so it had happened: Imran had been completely cured through medicine and without an operation.

I spent that first night with my family, and then the many nights and days that followed. After that I met friends and family who came from far and wide to visit me. People were not the only thing I'd missed during my imprisonment. I'd also missed the material things which I'd been prevented from seeing and feeling. I'd missed everyday things like glass and stone and wood – and different-coloured clothes after my five and a half years of orange suits. I was even eager to see fire and its flames.

I was beginning to regain my freedom and with it my humanity. Every time I went to the bathroom and locked the door, I felt incredibly happy. I was also overjoyed to walk unfettered. The darkness of night, of which I'd been deprived, was mine whenever I wanted it and with it I began to regain my sense of calm.

After a few days when my excitement began to subside and the sheer volume of visitors died down, I sat and made myself remember everything that had happened to me and all the torture and suffering that I'd undergone. I experienced a pressing need to cry out all the pains of the past, but when I tried to, I found I couldn't. My tears had dried up inside of me. I'd fought them back on so many occasions, not wanting the soldiers to think they could break me, and I'd refused to let go of my tears of joy at my release as I bid farewell to my imprisoned friends. I'd cried in the phone box on my own but I'd resisted joyful tears on my return to my family: I didn't want to sadden them. And now I found I couldn't cry.

I thought my tears had gone for ever. And then one day, when browsing a website that discussed the plight of prisoners in Guantánamo, I found a video of the children of my friend Shaker as they spoke about their father and called for his release. That's when I finally burst into tears. For them, and for their father, Shaker.

After that, I finally felt my chest begin to lighten.

Epilogue

A year after I was released, Allah blessed me with the birth of a baby girl. I named her Hanaan. Her presence makes me so happy. Whenever I look at her – and sometimes I just go and stare at the sight of my beautiful girl as she sleeps – I feel as if she'd somehow accompanied me through my suffering but was not given life until after I was released from prison. I hold her to my chest with such love. She marks the beginning of a new life and hope for me just as my release from prison was for her a means of her coming to life.

Yet I cannot forget the past. Just imagine: you're picked up for something you not only didn't do but had never even contemplated doing, and then, no matter how much you deny the charges against you, no one takes the slightest bit of notice. It's incomprehensible – even for one who lived through it.

I look back now on President Bush's words when he declared his 'war on terror' and I marvel at them. 'I also want to speak tonight directly to Muslims throughout the world,' he said. 'We respect your faith. It's practised freely by many millions of Americans, and by millions more in countries that America counts as friends. Its teachings are good and peaceful, and those who commit evil in the name of Allah blaspheme the name of Allah. The terrorists are traitors to their own faith, trying, in effect, to hijack Islam itself. The enemy of America is not our many Muslim friends; it is not our many Arab friends. Our enemy is a radical network of terrorists and every government that supports them.' Yet the fact that I was no radical terrorist made no difference to those who held me for more than five years.

In that same speech Bush continued: 'Our war on terror begins with al-Queda, but it does not end there. It will not end until every terrorist group of global reach has been found, stopped and defeated.' But there were no members of the IRA in Guantánamo, or of the Basque separatist group ETA, or of Sri Lanka's Tamil Tigers, or a whole host of other organisations that had used violence to try and achieve their ends. This wasn't because the American administration was shy about stealing people from countries other than Afghanistan or Pakistan: among my fellow prisoners were people who'd been picked up from Gambia, Georgia, Bosnia, and a variety of other Arab countries. What the prisoners of Guantánamo – and there were more than 750 prisoners of thirty-nine nationalities – had in common was that they were all Muslims. It was as if Bush, no matter his grand words, had equated Islam with terrorism.

'This is not, however, just America's fight,' Bush also said. 'And what is at stake is not just America's freedom. This is the world's fight. This is civilisation's fight. This is the fight of all who believe in progress and pluralism, tolerance and freedom.' Yet the reality of Guantánamo was the very opposite of progress, pluralism, tolerance and freedom.

Obama, during his election campaign, announced his intention to shut the camp and in the very first week of his presidency he reiterated that he'd end this saga of illegal detention by the beginning of 2010. It hasn't happened. As soon as he became commander-in-chief, Obama's statements became increasingly contradictory. On the one hand he claimed that the release of

Yemeni prisoners would pose a threat to America's security, and on the other he said that if he released these prisoners they might be subjected to torture. As if they weren't already being tortured! What really struck – and angered – me about these statements is that the president was repeating the very same words my interrogators had used.

As for me: the American military used me and they exploited me. They deprived me of my family, my life and my dignity. I'm convinced they must have known that I'd been a cook living in London but they wanted to keep me in Guantánamo and so they promoted me to a fantasy general from al-Qaeda. They claimed they had a witness to prove that I was trained in camps in Afghanistan in July 2001 but they never produced him. The only manner in which I was ever 'charged' was during the commission they set up to examine each prisoner's history. The list of allegations against me was laughable, from training camps and fatwas to being a member of an extremist group I'd never heard of and labelling as extremist mosques they'd never heard of. As for those charges: well, they could say what they liked. Since we were never intended to be prosecuted in public, they didn't need evidence.

I've experienced the pain of slavery, humiliation, brutality and torture; I grew used to the cruelty of Guantánamo's soldiers. I wonder whether history will record the story of the 'hostages of war' in the prison of Guantánamo Bay and the breaches by the American military, or whether it will shy away, turning a blind eye to the crimes committed there. I hope that this account, which is the truth of what happened to me, will help keep the world's eyes open.

Acknowledgements

I thank Allah for giving me the strength, ability and determination to write this book. It wasn't an easy thing to do: I had tried to forget Guantánamo and was reluctant to venture back into that darkness. But I knew I owed it to my fellow prisoners to write about what happened and so eventually, and with God's help, I did.

I want to thank Clive Stafford Smith who visited me in Guantánamo and who defended me and many of the other prisoners. Clive also came to my home in Tangier after I was released and he still keeps in touch. Thanks, too, to Chris Chang and all the staff and volunteers of Reprieve, whose tireless search proved to American intelligence that their allegations were false. Thanks to my agent, Anthony Sheil, who worked so hard to find a publisher and continues to give valuable support. Thanks also to Gillian Slovo, who helped complete and improve my book and has been so wonderful to work with, and to my editor, Becky Hardie, who made my writing clearer by showing me what a reader would want to know. And to Umar Geloo, the first person to volunteer to translate this book, free of charge, from Arabic, and Moazzam Begg who introduced me to Umar.

Acknowledgements

Finally, my very special thanks go to Jacquetta Wheeler who was one of the first to read my story and whose passion for it helped get it published. I am also grateful to Jacquetta's parents who opened their home to me.